STORRS LECTURES ON JURISPRUDENCE

Yale Law School, 2012

Cass R. Sunstein

Why

Yale UNIVERSITY PRESS

Nudge?

The Politics of Libertarian Paternalism

NEW HAVEN & LONDON

Published with assistance from the foundation established in memory of
Amasa Stone Mather of the Class of 1907, Yale College.

Copyright © 2014 by Cass R. Sunstein. All rights reserved.

This book may not be reproduced, in whole or in part, including illustrations,
in any form (beyond that copying permitted by Sections 107 and 108 of the U.S.
Copyright Law and except by reviewers for the public press), without written
permission from the publishers.

Yale University Press books may be purchased in quantity for educational, business,
or promotional use. For information, please e-mail sales.press@yale.edu (U.S.
office) or sales@yaleup.co.uk (U.K. office).

Set in Janson type by Integrated Publishing Solutions.
Printed in the United States of America.

The Library of Congress has cataloged the hardcover edition as follows:

Sunstein, Cass R.
Why nudge? : the politics of libertarian paternalism / Cass R. Sunstein.
pages   cm.— (Storrs lectures on jurisprudence)
Includes bibliographical references and index.
ISBN 978-0-300-19786-0 (hardback)
1. Paternalism—Political aspects—United States.   2. Libertarianism—United
States.   3. Consumer behavior—Political aspects—United States.   4. Choice
(Psychology)—Economic aspects—United States.   I. Title.
JC599.U5S94 2014
323.0973—dc23
2013035817

ISBN 978-0-300-21269-3 (pbk.)

A catalogue record for this book is available from the British Library.

10 9 8 7 6 5 4 3 2 1

For Eddie Bourke

The only purpose for which power can be rightfully exercised over any member of a civilized community, against his will, is to prevent harm to others. His own good, either physical or moral, is not a sufficient warrant. He cannot rightfully be compelled to do or forbear because it will be better for him to do so, because it will make him happier, because, in the opinion of others, to do so would be wise, or even right.

—John Stuart Mill, *On Liberty*

The central conundrum has been referred to as the Energy Paradox in this setting (and in several others). In short, the problem is that consumers appear not to purchase products that are in their economic self-interest. There are strong theoretical reasons why this might be so:

—Consumers might be myopic and hence undervalue the long-term.
—Consumers might lack information or a full appreciation of information even when it is presented.
—Consumers might be especially averse to the short-term losses associated with the higher prices of energy-efficient products relative to the uncertain future fuel savings, even if the expected present value of those fuel savings exceeds the cost (the behavioral phenomenon of "loss aversion").
—Even if consumers have relevant knowledge, the benefits of energy-efficient vehicles might not be sufficiently salient to them at the time of purchase, and the lack of salience might lead consumers to neglect an attribute that it would be in their economic interest to consider.

—U.S. Environmental Protection Agency,
Final Rule on Light-Duty Vehicle Greenhouse Gas
Emission Standards and Corporate Average
Fuel Economy Standards

Contents

Contents

Why Nudge?

Introduction: Behaviorally Informed Paternalism

On Wisconsin Avenue in Washington, DC, you can find a restaurant called The Daily Grill, which has created a special set of meals, known as Simply 600, on its lunch and dinner menus. All of those meals have six hundred calories or fewer. If you like, you can order the Chicken Marsala served over Angel Hair Pasta, or the Crab-Stuffed Salmon with Arugula and Grilled Tomato, or (my personal favorite) the Idaho Grilled Trout.

The Simply 600 menu is printed on a separate, highly visible section of the restaurant's larger menu. And right outside The Daily Grill, there is a large display featuring the phrase "Simply 600" in big characters, with appealing photographs of the various options on the special menu.

Is The Daily Grill being paternalistic? Maybe not. Maybe

it is merely catering to what people want, and letting its health-conscious customers know that it has what they are seeking. Maybe it believes that people's preferences are not static, and maybe it is seeking to alter those preferences in order to attract additional business. But maybe it believes that customers would be better off if they chose healthful, low-calorie meals, and maybe it is hoping to help customers to do exactly that, even if they would not choose such meals without a little help from The Daily Grill.

Suppose that as a matter of fact, the last explanation is the right one. On this account, the restaurant is not forcing anyone to choose anything. If people want high-calorie meals, they can get them, even at The Daily Grill. But the point of the Simply 600 menu is to make healthful choices salient and easy—and in that way to nudge consumers not merely to decide to have their meal at The Daily Grill, but also to make those very choices. If so, we appear to be dealing with a case of paternalism.

To be sure, the paternalism is mild, and it is not coming from the government. But if it is paternalistic, is it really objectionable as such? Would things be different, or worse, if governments adopted Simply 600 menus at their own cafeterias? Are things different, or worse, if government seeks to promote more healthful eating by requiring menus to contain calorie information, as indeed the Affordable Care Act does for chain restaurants and similar retail food establishments? What if the government embarks on an aggressive, even graphic educational campaign designed to promote healthful eating—or taxes unhealthful foods, as France, Finland, Denmark, Britain, Hungary, Ireland, and Romania have either done or seriously considered?

Paternalism stirs strong emotions. Many people abhor it. They think that human beings should be able to go their own way, even if they end up in a ditch. When they run risks, even foolish ones, it isn't anybody's business if they do. People have a right to be foolish. Paternalism is especially unwelcome if it comes from government. What gives public officials the right to interfere with the self-regarding decisions of adults, whether the subject is health, wealth, sex, or religion?

However controversial it was in the nineteenth century, the central argument of John Stuart Mill's *On Liberty* has numerous followers in the twenty-first. In his great and inspiring essay, Mill insisted that as a rule, government may not legitimately coerce people if its goal is to protect them from themselves.[1] In a defining passage, Mill contended that

the only purpose for which power may be rightfully exercised over any member of a civilized community, against his will, is to prevent harm to others. His own good, either physical or mental, is not a sufficient warrant. He cannot rightfully be compelled to do or forbear because it will be better for him to do so, because it will make him happier, because, in the opinion of others, to do so would be wise, or even right. . . . The only part of the conduct of anyone, for which he is amenable to society, is that which concerns others. In the part which merely concerns himself, his independence is, of right, absolute. Over himself, over his own body and mind, the individual is sovereign.[2]

This, then, is Mill's Harm Principle (sometimes called the Liberty Principle). Unless there is harm to others, the government cannot exercise power over people. The idea of "consumer sovereignty," central to modern economics and much political debate, is a close cousin to the Harm Principle. Even if Mill's own concerns seem to revolve around morals legislation, we should be able to see immediately that the Harm Principle raises serious doubts about many laws and regulations, including those that require people to get a prescription before obtaining certain medicines, forbid employees from working in unsafe workplaces (even if they would voluntarily run those risks), and promote food safety. In all of these cases, power is exercised over people in large part to promote their own good. When the resulting requirements are in place, people are not entirely sovereign over their own bodies and minds.

My goal in this book is to challenge the Harm Principle on the ground that in certain contexts, people are prone to error, and paternalistic interventions would make their lives go better. In these circumstances, there is a strong and emphatically *moral* argument on behalf of paternalism. I will also suggest that important influences on our behavior, in grave tension with the Harm Principle, are essentially inevitable, and to that extent, the principle cannot get off the ground. As we shall see, the Harm Principle would rule out many sensible practices that are now in effect, and it would forbid many potentially beneficial reforms. Of course it is exceedingly important to limit the power of government, and of course individuals often know best. Adults should not be treated like children. On those scores, Mill still has a great deal to teach us.[3] But since his time, we have learned a lot that he did not and could not know, especially about human error, and what we have learned cuts at some of the foundations of the Harm Principle.[4]

In the United States, Europe, and elsewhere, many people endorse the Harm Principle. They regard national nannies as annoying meddlers at best—and perhaps as tyrants. In every recent period, democratic nations have engaged in both theoretical and practical disputes about the legitimate boundaries of paternalism. Currently, there are heated controversies over measures meant to reduce smoking and to increase exercise, and also over the "food police," allegedly responsible for recent efforts to reduce the risks associated with obesity and unhealthful eating. The Simply 600 menu has not provoked much controversy, but if government tried to require or even to encourage it, a public outcry would be inevitable.

In the United States, public debates have erupted over apparently sensible (and life-saving) laws requiring people to buckle their seatbelts or to wear helmets while riding motorcycles. Many people believe that the "individual mandate" in the Affordable Care Act, which requires all adults to have health insurance, is a form of unacceptable paternalism.[5] The specific content of the disputes changes over time, but the fundamental issues endure. And in this domain, there are no simple partisan divisions. Paternalism is sometimes favored by those on the political left (perhaps seeking to improve people's diets) and sometimes by those on the right (perhaps seeking to encourage chastity or marriage).

In Mill's account, it is only when "there is definite damage, or a definite risk of damage, either to an individual or to the public," that "the case is taken out of the province of liberty and placed in that of morality or law."[6] Mill offered a number of independent justifications for the Harm Principle, but one of the most important is that individuals are in the best position to know what is good for them. In Mill's view, the problem with outsiders, including government officials, is that they lack the necessary information. Mill insists that because the individual "is the person most interested in his own well-being, the interest which any other person, except in cases of strong personal attachment, can have in it is trifling, compared with that which he himself has." Mill contends that "with respect to his own feelings and circumstances, the ordinary man or woman has means of knowledge immeasurably surpassing those that can be possessed by any one else."[7] When society seeks to overrule the individual's judgment, it does so on the basis of "general presumptions" that "may be altogether wrong, and even if right, are as likely as not to be misapplied to individual cases, by persons no better acquainted with the circumstances of such cases than those are who look at them merely from without."[8]

If the goal is to ensure that people's lives go well, Mill argues that the right solution is for public officials to allow people to find their own paths. Because individuals know their tastes and situations better than officials do, they are in the best position to identify their own ends and the best means of obtaining them.

Here, then, is an enduring argument, instrumental in character, on behalf of free markets and free choice in countless domains, including those in which people choose to run risks that may not turn out so well. Let us call this the Epistemic Argument for the Harm Principle. It has a great deal of force. In my view, it provides the strongest support that the Harm Principle can find. Of course there are other important arguments for the Harm Principle, involving human diversity, the importance of experimentation and learning over time, and the independent values of dignity and freedom of choice. We shall explore all of them in due course.

Choosing Well, Choosing Poorly

The Epistemic Argument has a great deal of intuitive appeal. But is it right? That is largely an empirical question, and it cannot be adequately answered by introspection, rhetoric, anecdotes, or intuitions. In recent decades, some of the most important research in social science, coming from psychologists and behavioral economists, has been trying to answer it. That research is having a significant influence not only on social science but also on public officials throughout the world.

Of course the human brain is a miraculous instrument, and individuals usually do make far better choices than those who seek to choose for them. But behavioral findings are creating serious problems for the Epistemic Argument, because they show that people make a lot of mistakes, some of which can prove extremely damaging.[9] Consider the instructive words of federal judge Richard Posner, a longtime critic of behavioral economics and a longtime advocate for the view that human beings are essentially rational:

What is called "behavioral economics" . . . has undermined the economic model of man as a rational maximizer of his self-interest and helped to expose the rampant exploitation by business of consumer psychology. Businesses know, and economists are learning, that consumers are easily manipulated by sellers into making bad choices—choices they would never make if they knew better—in borrowing and investing, and in buying goods and services, such as food, health care, and education.[10]

Human beings can be myopic and impulsive, giving undue weight to the short term (perhaps by smoking, or texting while driving, or eating too much chocolate).[11] What is *salient* greatly matters.[12] If an important feature of a situation, an activity, or a product lacks salience, people might ignore it, possibly to their advantage (perhaps because it is in the other room, and fattening) and possibly to their detriment (if it could save them money or extend their lives). Human beings procrastinate and sometimes suffer as a result.[13] They are greatly affected by default rules, which establish what happens if they do nothing. Because nothing is what many people will do, default rules can produce a lot of damage (or do a lot of good).[14] People can be unrealistically optimistic and for that reason make unfortunate and even dangerous choices.[15] They make "affective forecasting errors": They predict that activities or products will have certain beneficial or adverse effects on their well-being, but those predictions turn out to be wrong.[16]

It is important to emphasize that free markets provide significant protection against such errors. Competition may well deter businesses from trying to exploit our propensity to blunder. If companies provide unhelpful default rules, steering consumers in directions that harm them, they may be punished as a result of market competition. Who is going to trust such companies or keep doing business with them? Companies that hide expensive attributes, and thus cost consumers a lot of money, may eventually find themselves without customers. Much of the time, free markets are the best safeguards against cognitive errors.

In addition, companies offer countless services to help people counteract self-control problems. The free market creates strong incentives for companies to respond to these and other problems. With new technologies, those responses will become increasingly useful, frequent, inventive, and personalized.[17] If you have a problem with your weight, you can find a lot of help through devices that monitor your food consumption and give you clear advice about how to reach your goals. Useful software applications are proliferating,[18] and in the future we will see unimaginably more. The market for protecting people against their own mistakes is flourishing.[19] We can imagine a whole universe of behavioral apps, specifically designed to help people to counteract the mistakes to which they are prone.

But there is another side. Free markets may well reward sellers who attempt to exploit human errors. In identifiable cases, those who do *not* exploit human errors will be seriously punished by market forces, simply because their competitors are profiting from doing so. Credit markets provide many sad examples. Consider cell phone plans, credit card plans, checking accounts, and mortgages, which usually have many good features but which are often unfathomably complex, and which can hide potentially damaging terms (such as high fees for "overdraft protection").[20] In all of those areas, it is possible that companies that provide clear, simple products would do poorly in the marketplace, because they are not taking advantage of people's propensity to blunder.

Of course, a great deal remains to be understood about the nature and extent of human error in various contexts. We do know that people's behavior displays "ecological rationality," in the sense that we tend to choose well in environments for which our rules of thumb, or heuristics, are well suited.[21] Those environments are the norm, not the exception, and for that reason, our choices generally tend to be right for us. It makes far more sense to say that people display bounded rationality than to accuse them of "irrationality," and for many purposes, bounded rationality is just fine, producing outcomes that are equal to or perhaps even better than what would emerge from efforts to optimize by assessing all costs and benefits.

With respect to errors, more is being learned every day. Some behavioral findings remain highly preliminary and need further testing. There is much that we do not know. Randomized controlled trials, the gold standard for empirical research, must be used far more to obtain a better understanding of how the relevant findings operate in the world.[22] Even at this stage, however, the underlying findings have been widely noticed, and behavioral economics, cognitive and social psychology, and related fields have had a significant effect on policies in several nations, including the United States and the United Kingdom.

In the United States, many initiatives have been informed by behavioral findings. These initiatives enlist such tools as disclosure, warnings, and default rules, and they can be found in many areas, involving fuel economy, energy efficiency, environmental protection, health care, and obesity.[23] Indeed, behavioral findings are providing an important reference point for regulatory and other policymaking in the United States.[24]

In the United Kingdom, Prime Minister David Cameron created a Behavioural Insights Team with the specific goal of incorporating an understanding of human behavior into policy initiatives.[25] The official website states that its "work draws on insights from the growing body of academic research in the fields of behavioural economics and psychology which show how often subtle changes to the way in which decisions are framed can have big impacts on how people respond to them."[26] The Behavioural Insights Team has used this research to promote initiatives in numerous areas, including smoking cessation, energy efficiency, organ donation, consumer protection, charitable donation, and compliance strategies in general.[27] Other nations have expressed keen interest in its work, and its operations are expanding.[28] In 2013, the Obama administration created its own team to consider behavioral science and to bring empirical evidence to bear on government decisions.

Behavioral economics has drawn attention in Europe as a whole. For example, the Organisation for Economic Development and Cooperation (OECD) has published a Consumer Policy Toolkit that recommends a number of initiatives rooted in behavioral findings.[29] The European Union's Directorate-General for Health and Consumers has also shown the influence of behavioral economics.[30] *Green Behavior*, a report from the European Commission, enlists behavioral economics to outline policy initiatives to protect the environment.[31] Efforts to catalogue the large and growing set of behaviorally informed initiatives have called attention to "the Rise of the Psychological State."[32] This term is not the best advertising, because it seems a bit alarming; no one is likely to vote for a candidate who says that he supports "the Psychological State." But the term has the virtue of spotlighting efforts, all over the world, to develop sensible, low-cost policies with close reference to how human beings actually think and behave.

Choice Architecture

Findings about human error raise a natural question, which is whether an improved understanding of thought and behavior opens greater space for paternalism. Perhaps that understanding supplements the standard economic accounts of "market failure" by providing justifications for government action even without harm to others or some kind of collective action problem.[33] We do know that people are much affected by *choice architecture*, meaning the background against which choices are made.[34] Such architecture is both pervasive and inevitable, and it greatly influences outcomes, whether or not we are even aware of it. In fact choice architecture can be decisive. It effectively makes countless decisions for us, and it influences numerous others, by pressing us in one direction or another.[35] For example, do printers have single-sided or double-sided default settings? People use a lot more paper with a single-sided default.[36] Here as elsewhere, choice architecture cannot be avoided.

The great novelist David Foster Wallace began a speech with the following joke: "There are these two young fish swimming along, and they happen to meet an older fish swimming the other way, who nods at them and says, 'Morning, boys, how's the water?' And the two young fish swim on for a bit, and then eventually one of them looks over at the other and goes, 'What the hell is water?'"[37] This is of course a joke about choice architecture (fortunately, there aren't many). It is also instructive, because it puts a spotlight on a central fact of life, which is that central, even essential parts of the social background are so taken for granted that they are unnamed, unnoticed, and invisible. As we shall see, this point raises serious problems for the Harm Principle, because influences on our choices are omnipresent, and we may not even see them.

Choice architecture exists whenever we enter a cafeteria, a restaurant, a hospital, or a grocery store; when we select a mortgage, a car, a health care plan, or a credit card; when we turn on a tablet or a computer and visit our favorite websites (including government websites), which highlight some topics and downplay others; and when we apply for drivers' licenses or building permits or social security benefits. The Daily Grill certainly offers a choice architecture, and its Simply 600 menu is a form of such architecture. No restaurant lacks choice architecture, and any menu contains one. (Menus matter, for food as well as for candidates for public office, among other things because people are more likely to choose what is first.) In 1997, those who administered a college entrance exam increased the number of free reports that students could send to colleges (from three to four). As a result, students applied to many more places, and low-income students ended up attending more selective colleges, thus obtaining higher expected earnings over their lifetimes.[38]

For all of us, a key question is whether the choice architecture is helpful and simple, or harmful, complex, and exploitative. Any architecture will exercise power over the people who are subject to it. Since we cannot eliminate choice architecture, might violations of the Harm Principle turn out to be inevitable? Might Mill and his followers have missed the inevitable effects of that architecture?

This question raises others. Should choice architects, including those in the public sphere, be authorized to move people's decisions in their preferred directions? Would any such effort be unacceptably paternalistic? Who will monitor the choice architects, or create a choice architecture for them?[39] Economists have an elaborate account of the "market failures" that can justify government intervention, including monopoly, an absence of information on the part of consumers, and the harmful effects on third parties, such as pollution, that can come from voluntary agreements ("externalities"). But this account seems incomplete. The various empirical findings allow us to identify a set of *behavioral market failures*,[40] understood as market failures that complement the standard economic account and that stem from the human propensity to err. Is it unacceptably paternalistic to use such failures to justify regulation? Is it legitimate to use choice architecture to counteract behavioral market failures?

My basic answers are that choice architecture is inevitable and that behavioral market failures do, in fact, justify certain forms of paternalism.[41] When these failures occur and are significant, there are good (presumptive) reasons for a regulatory response even when no harm to others can be found. It should be clear that this position is rooted in a rejection of Mill's Epistemic Argument for the Harm Principle—not because the Epistemic Argument is always wrong, but because it is not always right.

While I mean to reject the Harm Principle here, there are important qualifications. No one should deny that government officials can also err, and their errors may be especially, even uniquely, damaging. Even the most benign paternalists can go badly wrong, and some paternalists are far from benign. In addition, people are highly diverse in terms of their tastes, their values, and their situations. One size may not fit all. In light of the pervasive risk of government error and the inescapable fact of human diversity, it is usually best to use the mildest and most choice-preserving forms of intervention. These forms include "nudges," understood as initiatives that maintain freedom of choice while also steering people's decisions in the right direction (as judged by people themselves).[42] The Simply 600 menu is certainly a nudge; so is a GPS. Nudges include disclosure of information, warnings, and appropriate default rules, which establish what happens if people do nothing at all. We might even venture a general principle, which might be called the First (and only) Law of Behaviorally Informed Regulation: *In the face of behavioral market failures, nudges are usually the best response, at least when there is no harm to others.*

Indeed, there is a plausible argument that paternalism of this limited kind does not run afoul of the Harm Principle.[43] Mill contended that while a person "cannot rightfully be compelled to do or forbear because it will be better for him to do so," there may nonetheless be "good reasons for remonstrating with him, or reasoning with him, or persuading him, but not for compelling him, or visiting him with any evil, in case he do otherwise."[44] Mill did not provide a full account of the paternalist's toolbox (see chapter 2), nor did he have a full sense of the nature and power of choice architecture, but at least some nudges fall comfortably within the category of remonstrating, reasoning, and persuading rather than compelling.

At the same time, there are exceptions to the First Law of Behaviorally Informed Regulation, and the choice of response depends on an analysis of the consequences for people's welfare, which requires a careful assessment of both costs and benefits.[45] In some cases, the best response may be none at all, because the costs exceed the benefits (just as no response may be best even when there is harm to others).[46] In other cases, stronger responses, even mandates, may turn out to be justified, because the benefits exceed the costs. Social welfare—a more capacious and open-ended term than "utility," emphasized by Mill—is the master concept, and it calls for attention to whether people are able to have good lives (by their own lights).

Freedom of choice is certainly a component of a good life, but in some cases, it can be overridden (as Mill himself acknowledged). When individual and social welfare appears to call for a stronger response than a mere nudge, we should give it serious consideration.[47] If laws that require people to buckle their seatbelts, or that prohibit them from texting while driving, are well justified on cost-benefit grounds, they should count as acceptable forms of paternalism.

Means vs. Ends, Hard vs. Soft

It is useful to begin, I suggest, by distinguishing among varieties of paternalism. Some varieties respect people's ends and try only to influence their choices of means. Other varieties attempt to affect people's choices of ends.

Means paternalists might help people to save money by requiring refrigerators to be more energy-efficient, when saving money is exactly what they want to do. Ends paternalists might forbid people from engaging in certain sexual activity, even though engaging in such activity is exactly what they want to do. Behavioral economists generally focus on means, not ends. Most of their key findings involve human errors with respect to means. Their goal is to create choice architecture that will make it more likely that people *will promote their own ends, as they themselves understand them.* And indeed, my focus here will be on means paternalism, not ends paternalism.

Moreover, some varieties of paternalism are highly aggressive, or "hard," while others are "soft." Soft paternalism is weaker and essentially libertarian, in the crucial sense that it preserves freedom of choice. In that respect, soft paternalism might be compatible with the Harm Principle, though we will see some serious complexities on that count. A jail sentence and a fine count as hard paternalism, whereas a disclosure policy, a warning, and a default rule count as soft or libertarian paternalism. Some forms of paternalism impose material costs, such as fines, on people's choices in order to improve their welfare. Other forms impose affective or psychic costs, as in the case of graphic health warnings, which might be designed to frighten people. Behavioral economists have generally favored soft rather than hard paternalism.[48] Means paternalism can be hard or soft, and the same is true of ends paternalism. My topic here extends far beyond libertarian paternalism and nudges, understood as approaches that affect choices without coercion, but it is important to see that nudges generally fall in the categories of means paternalism and soft paternalism.

Behavioral Market Failures

My central claim is simple: Behavioral market failures are an important supplement to the standard account of market failures, and in principle, they do justify (ideal) responses, even if those responses are paternalistic. In short, we need to add behavioral market failures to the class of justifications for government regulation, and the prospect of paternalism should not deter a careful inquiry, based on the likely consequences, into the appropriate response. As in the case of standard failures, however, the argument for a government response must be qualified by a recognition that public officials are fallible, that the cure may be worse than the disease, and that all relevant benefits and costs must be taken into account.

I emphasize five additional conclusions:

1. Choice architecture is inevitable, and hence certain influences on choices are also inevitable, whether or not they are intentional or the product of any kind of conscious design.

2. Some of the most intuitively appealing (and intensely felt) objections to paternalism are not epistemic. They rely on autonomy. They suggest that people have a right to decide for themselves, even if those decisions will go badly wrong. They point to the importance of human dignity. But as applied to most efforts to remedy behavioral market failures, those objections have little force, because those efforts do not interfere with autonomy or dignity, rightly understood. In fact, some of those efforts promote autonomy, in part because they open up time and resources for more pressing matters.[49] People are busy, and without a degree of paternalism, we would quickly be overloaded with the task of choice making, which would compromise our autonomy.

3. There is a serious risk that autonomy-based objections are rooted in a heuristic for what really matters, which is welfare. When people invoke autonomy and insist that people have a right to make their own mistakes, they might really be thinking that the Epistemic Argument is correct, and that

people know better than outsiders do (especially outsiders who work for the government). In short, those who invoke autonomy might be using a mental shortcut. Perhaps welfare is what really matters, and perhaps autonomy is important, at least in the cases at hand, not because it is a genuinely independent value but because people sometimes become frustrated and angry if they cannot get their own way—a point about welfare.

4. The most powerful and enduring objections to paternalism invoke welfare. The fear is that paternalist government will make people's lives worse, not better. These objections must be taken extremely seriously. In some contexts, they are a good place to start and even to end, especially insofar as they emphasize the importance of private learning, the fact of human diversity, and the risk of government error. The problem with these objections is that they depend on empirical claims that are often false. People are sometimes bad choosers, making their lives go worse (and get shorter). In some cases, public officials are in an excellent position to help. In many contexts, the objections to paternalism depend on strong empirical assumptions, involving extreme optimism about private choosers and extreme pessimism about public officials, that do not always hold. It follows that there is no sufficient abstract or a priori argument against paternalism, whether hard or soft.[50]

5. The strength of the objections to paternalism depends on the particular form that paternalism takes. The objections

are weakest when it is soft and limited to means. Especially in such cases, there are many opportunities for improving welfare without intruding on freedom of choice.

I have already suggested the upshot of these conclusions, which is that there is an emphatically moral argument for certain kinds of paternalism. Officials can make people's lives better if they are alert to behavioral market failures and design choice architectures that give health, wealth, and well-being the benefit of the doubt. Of course there are important questions, which I will engage in due course, about how to control the choice architects.

This book comes in five chapters. Chapter 1 discusses human errors, with particular emphasis on those errors that are most likely to matter for purposes of thinking about paternalism and its limits. Chapter 2 explores the nature of paternalism, distinguishing among various forms and emphasizing the wide range of tools that paternalistic choice architects might use. Chapter 3 turns to welfarist objections to paternalism, captured in the idea that people know what is best for them and outsiders do not. Chapter 4 explores autonomy and the objection that paternalism is an insult to people's right to choose. Chapter 5 discusses several independent objections to soft or libertarian paternalism, particularly those that emphasize the potential lack of transparency, the risk of manipulation, and the limits of the easy reversibility that soft paternalists prize.

Occasions for Paternalism

In recent decades, there has been an outpouring of empirical work on how human beings think and behave—and about the risk of serious error, especially in unusual or unfamiliar situations.[1] As I have noted, this work has been noticed by policymakers, and its influence is likely to grow. My goal in this chapter is to provide a brief summary, acknowledging that a great deal remains to be learned. My emphasis is on those findings that have special importance for the Harm Principle and the uses of paternalism.

Two Systems in the Mind:
Of Humans and Econs

Within recent social science, authoritatively discussed by Daniel Kahneman in his masterful *Thinking, Fast and Slow*, it has become standard to suggest that the human mind contains not one but two "cognitive systems."[2] In the social science literature, the two systems are unimaginatively described as System 1 and System 2. System 1 is the automatic system, while System 2 is deliberative and reflective. System 1 can be understood to reflect the behavior of Humans, whereas Econs think and act in accordance with System 2.[3]

System 1 works fast. It is often on automatic pilot. Driven by habits, it can be emotional and intuitive. When it hears a loud noise, it is inclined to run. When it is offended, it wants to hit back. It certainly eats a delicious brownie. It can procrastinate; it can be impulsive. It wants what it wants when it wants it. It can be excessively fearful and too complacent. It is a doer, not a planner. System 1 is a bit like Homer Simpson, James Dean from *Rebel Without a Cause*, and Pippi Longstocking.

System 2 is more like a computer or Mr. Spock from the old *Star Trek* show (or the android Data from the somewhat less old *Star Trek* show). It is deliberative. It calculates. When it hears a loud noise, it assesses whether the noise is a cause for concern. It thinks about probability, carefully though sometimes slowly. It does not really get offended. If it sees reasons for offense, it makes a careful assessment of what, all things considered, ought to be done. It sees a delicious brownie and makes a judgment about whether, all things considered, it should eat it. It insists on the importance of self-control. It is a planner as well as a doer; it does what it has planned.

These points raise some natural questions. What, exactly, are these systems? Are Humans and Econs agents? Do they operate as homunculi in the brain? Are they little people? Are they actually separate? In the case of conflict, who adjudicates?

The best answer is that the idea of two systems is a heuristic device, a simplification that is designed to distinguish between automatic, effortless processing and more complex, effortful processing. When people are asked to add one plus one, or to walk from their bedroom to their bathroom in the dark, or to read the emotion on the face of their best friend, the mental operation is easy and rapid. When people are asked to multiply 179 times 283, navigate a new neighborhood by car, or decide which retirement or health insurance plan best fits their needs, the mental operation is difficult and slow.

Identifiable regions of the brain are active in different tasks, and hence it may well be right to suggest that the idea of "systems" has physical referents. An influential discussion contends that "automatic and controlled processes can be roughly distinguished by where they occur in the brain."[4] The prefrontal cortex, the most advanced part of the brain (in evolutionary terms) and the part that most separates human beings from other species, is associated with deliberation and hence with System 2. The amygdala has been associated with a number of automatic processes, including fear,[5] and it can thus be associated with System 1.

Consider the question of whether people pay sufficient attention to their own futures. This is an especially important topic for assessing paternalism, because public officials are often concerned that people enjoy short-term benefits (from smoking, spending, or overeating) at the expense of long-term harm. Econs give due consideration to the long term, but Humans may well ignore it, and when they do, perhaps we have an occasion for paternalism.

Neuroscientists have actually located a part of the brain—the ventromedial pFC (vMPFC)—that is most active when people are thinking about themselves. (If you want to have a narcissistic moment and focus on yourself right now, your vMPFC will be active.) By itself, perhaps, that is not so interesting. But neuroscientists have also found that when impatient people are thinking about their future selves, the vMPFC is not active.[6] In patient people, by contrast, that region of the brain *is* active when they are thinking of their future selves.[7] Here, then, is a neurological basis for distinguishing between Humans and Econs. Impatient people think of their future selves in the same way that they think of strangers—raising the possibility that they may not be sufficiently concerned about their own future well-being.

On the other hand, different parts of the brain interact, and it would be hazardous to locate System 1 and System 2 in particular regions. Fortunately, there is no need to make technical or controversial claims about neuroscience in order to distinguish between effortless and effortful processing. The idea of System 1 and System 2 is designed to capture that distinction in a way that works for purposes of exposition (and that can be grasped fairly immediately by System 1).

Here is a striking demonstration of the relationship between the two systems. Behavioral economists have shown that people are affected by how a problem is "framed." Suppose that you are deciding whether to have an operation. You are far more likely to have that operation if you are told that of a hundred people who have the operation, ninety are alive after five years than if you are told that after five years, ten are dead. The purely semantic reframing has a major effect on people's judgments. Similarly, people are "loss averse," in the sense that they dislike losses more than they like corresponding gains. If people face a five-cent tax for using a plastic bag (a loss), they are much more likely to be affected than if they are given a five-cent bonus (a gain) for bringing their own bag.[8] In response to questions, people persistently show both framing effects and loss aversion. (There is a nice lesson here for policymakers. If you want to have an impact, choose effective frames and enlist loss aversion. Is it paternalistic for policymakers to heed that lesson? Before you answer "yes," note that some kind of framing is inevitable.)

Now assume that people are answering those same questions in a foreign language—that is, a language that they speak, but in which they are not entirely comfortable. Here is the key finding: It turns out that they do not show either framing effects or loss aversion.[9] Asked to resolve problems in a language that is not their own, people are less likely to depart from standard accounts of rationality. In an unfamiliar language, they are more likely to get the right answer. How can this be?

The answer is straightforward. When people are using their own language, they think quickly and effortlessly, so System 1 has the upper hand. But when people are using another tongue, System 1 gets a bit overwhelmed and may even be rendered inoperative, while System 2 is given a serious boost. Our rapid, intuitive reactions are slowed down when we are using a language with which we are not entirely familiar. We are more likely to do some calculating and to think deliberatively—and at least on some questions, to give the right answers. In a foreign language, people have some distance from their intuitions and their emotions, and that distance can stand them in good stead. In a foreign language, Humans recede in favor of Econs.

As the authors of the relevant study write, "Perhaps the

most important mechanism for our effect is the reduction in emotional resonance that is associated with using a foreign language. . . . An emotional reaction sometimes induces a less systematic decision."[10] Compare the choice of Samuel Beckett, the Irish novelist and playwright, to write some of his greatest works in French rather than English, a decision that was rooted in a judgment that the less familiar language would promote greater clarity and force him to write more economically and to think more fundamentally.[11]

There is a lesson here about the importance of using less intuitive, more technical approaches to law and regulation, including those that emphasize the need to assemble information about costs and benefits and to give careful consideration to that information.[12] Such approaches do not (exactly) use a foreign language, but they do ensure that people have a degree of distance from their initial judgments, thus reducing the mistakes associated with System 1. People do not naturally think about regulation (involving, say, the environment, occupational safety and health, or terrorism) in terms of costs and benefits, but the effort to do so can weaken or eliminate the effect of intuitions, in a way that leads to greatly improved decisions. There is also a point here about the hazards of relying on our intuitions as a foundation for political or moral theory, including our thinking about paternalism—a point to which I will return.

The defining feature of System 1 is that it is automatic, but

System 1 can also be emotional, and its emotional character creates both risks and opportunities. People may be immediately fearful of some risk—say, the risk associated with terrorism, or the risk of losses in the stock market—whether or not reality, and the relevant statistics, suggest that there is cause for alarm. (Recall the importance of loss aversion; people can get pretty emotional about losses, even small ones.) A great deal of research finds that people tend to assess products, activities, and other people through "an affect heuristic."[13] When the affect heuristic is at work, people evaluate benefits, costs, and probabilities not by running the numbers but by consulting their feelings. They might hate coal-fired power plants or love nuclear power, and those feelings may influence their judgments about the benefits and costs of coal-fired power plants and nuclear power. System 1 is doing the key work here.

In fact, some goods and activities come with an "affective tax" or an "affective subsidy," in the sense that people like them more, or less, because of the affect that accompanies them. Advertisers and public officials try to create affective taxes and subsidies, which are an important part of choice architecture; consider public educational campaigns designed to reduce smoking or texting while driving. Some political campaigns have the same goal, attempting to impose a kind of affective tax on the opponent and to enlist the affect heuristic in their favor. Many political campaigns appeal directly to System 1.

The same is true for some lawyers involved in trials or even appellate litigation. If System 1 can be enlisted, it may run the show, with System 2 operating as a kind of ex post helper.[14] In many cases, System 2 acts as the lawyer, and System 1 is a most demanding client.

The affect heuristic is, of course, merely one of a large number of mental shortcuts that people use to make judgments. These shortcuts generally work well, which is why people use them, but they can also misfire. As I have noted, heuristics tend to have "ecological rationality," in the sense that they make sense in the settings where they are usually applied. Nonetheless, they can create major problems in new or unfamiliar settings.

When people use heuristics, they avoid answering a hard question and answer a simpler one instead.[15] For risks, people may not ask, "What is the statistical likelihood of harm?" (a potentially complex question) but instead, "Have I heard of any cases in which the potential harm actually came to fruition?" For political candidates, people may not ask, "Do I agree with Candidate *A* or Candidate *B* on economic policy?" (a potentially complex question) but instead, "Do I like and trust this person" or "Is this person like me?" (much easier questions).[16] Something similar is at work in educational campaigns that attempt to trigger fear (in the context, for example, of smoking, obesity, and texting while driving), and thus engage System 1 rather than offer statistical analyses.

In an interesting and important passage, Mill offered two exceptions to the Harm Principle, both connected with the operations of System 2. The first involves people below the age of adulthood; the second involves primitive peoples, whom Mill describes as living in "those backward states of society in which the race itself may be considered as in its nonage."[17] Mill concluded that "[d]espotism is a legitimate mode of government in dealing with barbarians, provided the end be their improvements, and the means justified by actually effecting that end. Liberty, as a principle, has no application to any state of things anterior to the time when mankind have become capable of being improved by free and equal discussion." Whatever we think of this passage, which raises obvious questions about parochialism and condescension, it is clear that Mill prizes System 2 and the opportunities for reflection, planning, calculation, and self-control that it affords.[18]

Behavioral Market Failures

I now turn to four sets of mistakes that produce significant harms and problems, and that should be counted as behavioral market failures. As we shall see, all of them are firmly rooted in the operations of System 1. With respect to paternalism, the unifying theme is that insofar as people are making the relevant errors, their choices will fail to promote their own ends. It follows that a successful effort to correct these errors would generally substitute an official judgment for that of choosers only with respect to means, not ends.[19]

There are, however, some complexities in this claim. The distinction between means and ends raises a number of difficult puzzles, some of them involving the identification of people's ends over time.

PRESENT BIAS, TIME INCONSISTENCY, AND SELF-CONTROL

According to standard economic theory, people will consider both the short and long term. They will take account of relevant uncertainties, including the potential unpredictability of the future and the possibility of significant changes over time. It may well be far better to have money, or a good event, a week from now than a decade from now. People may, rationally and reasonably, select different balances between the present and the future. With respect to present and future consumption, people who are twenty-five make different trade-offs from people who are sixty-five, and for excellent reasons.

In practice, however, some people procrastinate or neglect to take steps that impose small, short-term costs but would produce large, long-term gains. At least some of the relevant actions seem hard to justify.[20] While System 2 considers the long term, System 1 is myopic, and in multiple ways, people show *present bias*.[21] People may, for example, delay enrolling in a retirement plan,[22] starting to exercise, ceasing to smoke, or using some valuable, cost-saving technology.[23] Inertia is often exceedingly powerful,[24] and it helps account for the power of default rules, which establish what happens if people do nothing. Often nothing is exactly what people will do, so the default rule tends to stick, whether it involves saving for retirement, personal privacy, or clean energy.

For example, some of us decline to choose more energy-efficient products, including appliances and cars with good fuel economy, even when that choice would save us a lot of money. Many people make choices that have short-term net benefits but long-term net costs, including a significant risk of causing premature death (as is the case, for many, with smoking cigarettes and poor diet). Procrastination, inertia, hyperbolic discounting,[25] and associated problems of self-control[26] are especially troublesome when the result is a small short-term gain at the expense of large long-term losses. There is a close connection between procrastination and myopia, understood as an excessive focus on the short term.

Time inconsistency arises when people's preferences at Time 1 diverge from their preferences at Time 2.[27] At Time 1, people might prefer to eat a great deal, smoke, spend, become angry, drink, procrastinate, or gamble. The resulting choices might have serious harmful effects at Time 2, making their lives far worse. Recall that an identifiable region of the brain is most actively engaged when people are thinking about themselves, but for impatient people in particular, this region is less active when they are thinking about their future selves.[28] Psychologist Jason Mitchell and his coauthors contend that such "shortsighted decision-making occurs in part because people fail to consider their future interests as belonging to the self."[29] For those shortsighted people, the "vMPFC response was nearly identical when people tried to predict their future enjoyment . . . and another person's present enjoyment," suggesting that such people think of their own future selves in the same way that they think of strangers.[30]

Strikingly, Mitchell and his coauthors find that

the magnitude of this vMPFC difference between judgments of present and future enjoyment predicted the impatience or shortsightedness of people's intertemporal choices. Those participants in whom vMPFC activity *most* differentiated between predictions of present and future enjoyment tended to make the most impatient decisions, preferring small present rewards to large future rewards. In contrast, participants in whom vMPFC did not differentiate between predictions of present and future enjoyment tended to make the most patient decisions, preferring large future rewards to small present rewards.[31]

Consider in this regard problems of "internalities"[32]— problems of self-control and errors in judgment that harm the people who make those judgments. We can think of internalities as occurring when we make choices that injure our future selves. Of course, people can use various techniques to overcome this problem, including precommitment strategies; Ulysses' effort to protect himself from the Sirens is a famous example.[33] At the national level, constitutions can be understood as precommitment strategies, as those who ratify a constitution seek to protect themselves against their own future mistakes. For individuals, private markets are perfectly capable of creating products and practices to help overcome self-control problems; in fact, there are countless such products and practices. But it is at least plausible to suggest that regulatory approaches that address internalities can produce large welfare gains, and even save lives, by strengthening the authority of System 2.[34]

Such approaches might take the form of disclosure requirements or warnings designed to promote self-control. Flexible approaches of this kind have the advantage of maintaining freedom of choice and thus respecting diversity. Freedom of choice is important, not least because reasonable people should be allowed to trade off present and future in ways that suit their own situations. But we can imagine cases where an economic incentive or a mandate might be the best solution. Consider, for example, bans on texting while driving, if understood to protect drivers (as well as those whom they endanger). With respect to internalities, energy policy includes many examples, such as energy-efficiency requirements for appliances and fuel-economy requirements for vehicles.[35] Choice-preserving approaches are usually preferable, but under imaginable assumptions about costs and benefits, the best approach to a palpable neglect of the future might turn out to be a mandate or a ban.[36]

IGNORING SHROUDED
(BUT IMPORTANT) ATTRIBUTES

What do people notice? What do they miss? The social scientists Christopher Chabris and Daniel Simons tried to make some progress on these questions by asking people to watch a ninety-second movie, in which six ordinary people pass a basketball to one another.[37] The simple task? To count the total number of passes.

After the little movie is shown, the experimenter asks people how many passes they were able to count. Then the experimenter asks: *And did you see the gorilla?* A lot of people laugh at the question. *What gorilla?* Then the movie is replayed. Now that you are not counting passes, you see a gorilla enter the scene, plain as day, pound its chest and leave. The gorilla (actually a person dressed up in a gorilla suit) is not at all hard to see. In fact you can't miss it. But when counting passes, many people (typically about half) do miss it.

Behavioral economists have been quite interested in the gorilla experiment, because it shows that people are able to pay attention to only a limited number of things, and that when some of those things are not salient, we ignore them, sometimes to our detriment. Magicians and used-car dealers try to hide gorillas. Sometimes the same is true of those who provide credit cards, cell phone service, and mortgages, with terms that may well matter but that people do not notice.[38]

Attention is a scarce resource, and it is triggered by salience; it follows that salience greatly matters. One reason is that System 1 does not closely survey all aspects of social situations, and System 2 may be working hard on other business. When certain features of a product or an activity are not salient, people may disregard them even if they are important, and the result may cause them harm. Complexity and information overload are problems in part because of the importance of salience. When hidden amid complexity, important features of products and situations can be missed, creating real problems. In fact a lack of salience can be a serious kind of behavioral market failure.

Why, for example, do so many people pay bank overdraft fees? One answer is that such fees are not sufficiently salient to people, and some fees are incurred as a result of inattention and neglect. A careful study suggests that limited attention is indeed a source of the problem and that once overdraft fees become salient, they are significantly reduced.[39] When people take surveys about these fees, they are less likely to incur a fee in the following month, and when they take a number of surveys, the issue becomes sufficiently salient that overdraft fees are reduced for as much as two years.[40]

In many areas, the mere act of being surveyed can affect behavior—for example, by increasing use of water-treatment products (thus promoting health) and the take-up of health insurance. One reason is that being surveyed increases the salience of the action in question.[41] A field experiment finds that simple textual reminders that loan payments are due have a significant effect on payments—the same effect as a 25 percent decrease in interest![42] Another field experiment shows that reminders have a strong effect on people who are due for a dental checkup.[43] Personalized emails have been shown to be highly effective in promoting donations to charity.[44] Reminders and checklists are highly effective in part because they promote salience.

A more general point is that many nontrivial costs (or benefits) are less salient than purchase prices. They are "shrouded attributes" to which some consumers do not pay much attention. Such "add-on" costs may matter a great deal but receive little or no consideration because they are not salient.[45] A failure of attention to energy costs, which may be shrouded for some consumers, has significant implications for regulatory policy. Contrary to the Harm Principle, it suggests the potential benefits of mild forms of paternalism. The clearest implication is that people should be provided with cost-related information that they can actually understand. In 2011, the

Department of Transportation and the Environmental Protection Agency produced new fuel-economy labels with this goal in mind; the new labels explicitly draw attention to the economic benefits of greater fuel economy.[46]

An understanding of the problem of shrouded attributes also helps to identify a potential justification for regulatory standards in the domains of fuel economy and energy efficiency, involving a behavioral market failure. Of course, such standards reduce social costs by cutting air pollution and promoting energy security. To the extent that they reduce these costs, they do not involve paternalism in any way. But most of the benefits from recent rules are private; they come from consumer savings.[47] Here is where paternalism becomes relevant. On standard economic grounds, it is not simple to identify a market failure that would justify taking account of such benefits.

After all, people can buy fuel-efficient vehicles if they want. The fact that they are not buying such vehicles suggests that they do not want them. Isn't the government's emphasis on consumer savings a form of paternalism—producing a more fuel-efficient fleet than people demand? True, fuel-economy rules also produce benefits in the form of time savings. If cars get better gas mileage, people do not have to go to the gas station so often. But can't consumers figure that out for themselves?

The most plausible response is behavioral. The basic idea

is that when purchasing cars, people may not give sufficient attention to the long-term or aggregate costs. Of course the information is available, and most people do not ignore it, but many consumers might give the potential savings less weight than they deserve, if their goal is to save money on balance. Assume that if consumers paid a little more at the time of purchase, they could save a lot over the life of the vehicle (without sacrificing in terms of safety or other vehicle attributes). Why wouldn't they do that? The behavioral argument is that if they are well-designed, fuel-economy and energy efficiency standards will produce a set of outcomes akin to those that the market would produce if relevant attributes were not shrouded. To be sure, most people know that fuel and energy savings matter, and a lot of empirical work would be necessary to establish that the behavioral argument is right—and to confirm the existence of behavioral market failures here— but the behavioral argument does provide the best defense of existing rules.

This point has not escaped official attention. In explaining the new fuel-economy rules issued in 2012, the Department of Transportation referred to

> phenomena observed in the field of behavioral economics, including loss aversion, inadequate consumer attention to long-term savings, or a lack of salience of relevant benefits (such as fuel savings, or time savings associated

with refueling) to consumers at the time they make purchasing decisions. Both theoretical and empirical research suggests that many consumers are unwilling to make energy-efficient investments even when those investments appear to pay off in the relatively short-term. This research is in line with related findings that consumers may undervalue benefits or costs that are less salient, or that they will realize only in the future.[48]

So justified, fuel economy standards are a form of hard paternalism, and not easy to defend in terms of the Harm Principle, but those who favor such standards need not question people's ends. The idea is that people want to minimize all relevant costs, and if they are not taking account of some costs, properly designed fuel-economy standards promote, and do not override, their ends. It is true that if the problem is a lack of attention and salience, the most natural and presumptively appropriate response is disclosure, not a mandate—and on one view, fuel-economy labels, and not a mandate, are the better option. But if such a mandate has benefits far in excess of its costs, it would appear to be justified as well.[49]

UNREALISTIC OPTIMISM

System 2 is realistic, but System 1 is not.[50] A great deal of work in psychology and behavioral economics suggests that most people are unrealistically optimistic, in the sense that their predictions about their own behavior and prospects are systematically skewed in the optimistic direction.[51] Indeed, the tendency toward unrealistic optimism seems to be hardwired.[52] About 80 percent of the population tends to show unrealistic optimism, and the realists who make up the other 20 percent include a number of people who are clinically depressed.

Unrealistic optimism has significant benefits, because it can spur activity, lift spirits, promote resilience, and ensure that people continue to try even in tough circumstances. But it can have bad consequences as well, above all by leading to insufficient precautions. If people are unduly optimistic about their future behavior, they may select financial packages (say, for credit cards, mortgages, health care plans, and cell phones) that cause significant economic losses.[53] In addition, they may run risks (say, by texting while driving) that can lead to serious harm. If people are unduly optimistic, they may fail to take steps to reduce serious dangers. An obvious response is a disclosure strategy, perhaps including graphic warnings, that helps to counteract unrealistic optimism.[54]

When people imagine their own future, they tend to see it as very good, even if the likely reality is far more mixed.[55] The "above average" effect is common;[56] many people believe that they are less likely than others to suffer various misfortunes, including automobile accidents and bad health outcomes. One study found that while smokers do not underestimate the statistical risks faced by the population of smokers, they none-theless believe that their personal risk is less than that of the average nonsmoker.[57] Unrealistic optimism is related to con-firmation bias, which occurs when people give special weight to information that confirms their antecedent beliefs.[58] If peo-ple show that bias, and if it affects their behavior, they may be led in directions that produce serious losses.

What makes people unrealistically optimistic? How can they maintain such optimism in the face of repeated encoun-ters with reality, which should press them in the direction of greater realism? One answer involves a remarkable asym-metry in how we process information.[59] In brief, people give more weight to good news than to bad news.

The neuroscientist Tali Sharot and her collaborators find that when people receive information that is better than ex-pected, they are likely to change their beliefs accordingly—but that when they receive information that is worse than expected, their beliefs are far less likely to be affected. In the first stage of Sharot's experiment, people were asked to esti-mate their likelihood of experiencing eighty bad life events (such as robbery and Alzheimer's disease). In the second stage, they were given accurate information about the average prob-ability for similarly situated people. In the third stage, they were asked to state their views about their personal probability in light of what they had learned.

The central finding is that people were significantly more

likely to update their views when they got good news than when they got bad news. More specifically, people were more likely to move their personal probability estimate in a positive direction when they learned that the population average was above the number they gave than to move their personal probability estimate in a negative direction when they learned that the population average was below the number they gave. This is clear evidence of selective updating.[60]

Sharot and her coauthors also studied fMRI data to explore what happens in the brain—more particularly, in the inferior prefrontal gyrus (IFG), a region of the prefrontal cortex. The IFG is the region that corrects errors in estimation. Does it react differently to negative than to positive information? The answer is yes. The authors' basic conclusions are technical but worth quoting:

> We found that optimism was related to diminished coding of undesirable information about the future in a region of the frontal cortex (right IFG) that has been identified as being sensitive to negative estimation errors. Participants with high scores on trait optimism were worse at tracking undesirable errors in this region than those with low scores. In contrast, tracking of desirable information in regions processing desirable estimation errors (MFC/SFG, left IFG and cerebellum) did not differ between high and low optimists.[61]

A subsequent study found that people's ability to incorporate bad news into their judgments can be improved by disrupting the functioning of the left (but not the right) interior frontal gyrus; this disruption eliminates the good news/bad news effect.[62] The conclusion, with neural foundations, is that people are unrealistically optimistic in the particular sense that they are far more responsive to desired than to undesired information—a point that obviously raises challenges for regulatory policy and disclosure requirements in particular. Perhaps the most important point is that disclosure requirements may turn out to be ineffective with respect to optimistically biased consumers. Any such requirements should be devised so as to reduce that risk. Graphic warnings, grabbing the attention of System 1, are a possibility here.

PROBLEMS WITH PROBABILITY

System 1 does not handle probability well. One problem is the availability heuristic. When people use that heuristic, they make judgments about probability by asking whether a recent event comes readily to mind.[63] If an event is cognitively "available," people might well overestimate the risk. If an event is not cognitively available, they might underestimate the risk.[64]

In deciding whether it is dangerous to walk in a city at night, to text while driving, or to smoke, people often ask about incidents of which they are aware. While System 2 might be willing to do some calculations, System 1 works quickly, and it is pretty simple to use the availability heuristic. Instead of asking hard questions about statistics, System 1 asks easy questions about what comes to mind. "Availability bias" can lead to significant mistakes about the probability of bad outcomes, taking the form of either excessive fear or unjustified complacency.[65]

A distinct but related finding is that people sometimes do not make judgments on the basis of the expected value of outcomes, and they may neglect the central issue of probability, particularly when emotions are running high.[66] In such cases, people may focus on the outcome and not on the probability that it will occur.[67] If there is a small chance of catastrophe—the loss of a child, a fatal cancer—the outcome may dominate people's thoughts, rather than the statistical likelihood that it will happen. And if there is a small chance of having something wonderful—the best vacation ever or a fabulous job opportunity—people's enthusiasm about that outcome may crowd out the statistics. (This is one reason that state lotteries can be so popular.)

People who sell insurance trade on the public's fear of the worst-case scenarios. So do terrorists, who aim to convince civilians that they "cannot be safe anywhere." When people are making mistakes about probability, well-designed disclosure strategies, including warnings, could help. Here too, the government would be respecting people's ends. When officials (or private institutions) correct people's mistakes about risks, they are helping people to achieve their ends. But as we shall see, the distinction between means and ends raises puzzles of its own.

TWO

The Paternalist's Toolbox

Do the findings just outlined justify paternalism? The initial task is to produce a working definition of paternalism.

However it is defined, paternalism can come from diverse people and institutions. Employers, teachers, doctors, lawyers, architects, bankers, chefs, rental car companies, and countless others are capable of paternalism. All of these, and many others, may attempt to influence System 1 or educate System 2, and those efforts, along with social pressures, can greatly affect individual choices. We have seen that with its Simply 600 menu, The Daily Grill may well have been engaging in a form of paternalism, and there are countless examples in the same vein. My focus here, however, is on paternalism from government. (Mill's focus was much broader.)

Though the underlying issues deserve careful attention, and though my discussion bears directly on those issues, I do not explore behavioral justifications for paternalism from non-governmental actors.[1]

There are many recent examples of arguable or actual paternalism from public officials. Consider, for example, the highly controversial decision in 2012, initiated by New York Mayor Michael Bloomberg, to ban the sale (in certain places) of sodas in containers of more than sixteen ounces.[2] Mayor Bloomberg sought to reduce obesity, and he believed that the ban would promote that goal. Some people choose drinks in large containers, and Mayor Bloomberg's proposal would not merely influence that choice but make it unavailable. Much of the negative reaction to the proposal stemmed from the view that it was paternalistic and unacceptable for that reason. Why—critics asked and sometimes raged—should Mayor Bloomberg, rather than consumers themselves, decide the size of soft drink containers? His proposal was certainly taken as a form of paternalism. Note that it was a mild form. People could still drink as much as they like; they simply had to buy two containers rather than one. (I will turn below to the question of how best to characterize it, and also to whether it was a good idea. Short answer: Everything depends on its costs and benefits; the costs seem low, but the benefits are pretty speculative.)

Choices and Welfare

It is tempting to suggest that *the government acts paternalistically when it overrides people's choices on the ground that their choices will not promote their own welfare.* Mill spoke in similar terms, objecting to "the evil of allowing others to constrain" a person "to what they deem his good."[3] Mill would not forbid efforts to "aid his judgments, exhortations to strengthen his will," which "may be offered to him, even obtruded on him." The problem lies in coercing, controlling, and constraining.

But there is an immediate problem with this suggestion. The idea of "overriding" (like that of "coercing" or "constraining") is ambiguous. Government has a series of tools for influencing people. Some of the strongest involve incapacitation, with capital punishment and life imprisonment as the extreme cases. Insofar as we are speaking of these penalties, and of imprisonment more generally, it may be fair to speak of overriding choices. But other tools are more subtle, ranging from large and small monetary penalties to the use of education, warnings, default rules, and time, place, and manner restrictions. Even criminal and civil bans are often accompanied by monetary penalties, and if they are small, are choices really being "overridden"?

When the government imposes penalties on certain choices, it puts people who make those choices at some kind of risk or in some kind of jeopardy. Strictly speaking, choices are not overridden. If people are told that they will have to pay a fine if they engage in certain behavior, they remain free to engage in that behavior and to pay the fine. Paternalistic policies may influence rather than override choices. The idea of "overriding" choices is thus ambiguous and too restrictive.

The unifying theme of paternalistic approaches, however diverse, is that *government does not believe that people's choices will promote their welfare, and it is taking steps to influence or alter people's choices for their own good.*[4] In acting paternalistically, government may be attempting (1) to affect outcomes without affecting people's actions or beliefs; (2) to affect people's actions without influencing their beliefs; (3) to affect people's beliefs in order to influence their actions; or (4) to affect people's preferences, independently of affecting their beliefs, in order to influence their actions.

Automatic enrollment (for instance, in a savings or health insurance plan) would fall in the first category insofar as it affects outcomes but need not lead to any change in people's actions or beliefs; indeed, the power of automatic enrollment stems from the fact that it works when people do nothing. A civil fine would fall in the second category insofar as it affects what people do without necessarily affecting what they believe.[5] An educational campaign or a set of factual warnings, specifically designed to alter beliefs, would fall in the third. A graphic warning campaign about tobacco or distracted driving, designed to affect people's preferences, but without necessarily affecting their beliefs,[6] would fall in the fourth category.

Fervent opponents of paternalism may find all of these efforts objectionable, but for different reasons. For example, efforts to affect people's preferences might seem especially insidious except insofar as such efforts are limited to the provision of truthful information. Provision of information is certainly a nudge, but it may or may not qualify as paternalistic; I will explore that complex issue below.

What's Hard? What's Soft?

Let us dispense with the idea of "overriding" choices and explore the different tools that paternalistic officials might use. We can imagine attempts by government to improve people's welfare by threatening to *imprison* those who make certain choices. We can imagine attempts to improve people's welfare by threatening to *fine* those who make certain choices. If the government imposes criminal or civil fines on those who smoke marijuana, refuse to buckle their seatbelts, or gamble, and if it does so because it wants to influence people's choices in order to promote their own welfare, it is acting paternalistically. The same conclusion would certainly follow if people value their short-term satisfaction more highly than the government does.

There is of course a continuum here from paternalistic actions that impose high costs to those that impose low costs. A tiny monetary fine falls within the definition of paternalism, but it is not exactly an aggressive step. Note, however, that some sanctions have *expressive functions* and may be highly effective for that reason, even if the actual size of the sanction is small.[7] A modest criminal fine (say, for smoking, failing to buckle one's seatbelt, texting while driving, or gambling) may have a large deterrent effect. A paternalistic intervention with such a sanction, however modest, might be highly objectionable to those who abhor paternalism.

I have noted that even very small costs—say, a five-cent charge for a bag at a grocery store—may have a big effect on behavior. A careful analysis shows such an effect, in part because of the power of loss aversion.[8] If such small costs are imposed in order to protect people against their own bad or harmful choices, the decision to impose them counts as paternalistic. A tiny fine—say, a one-cent charge—would not qualify as highly coercive, but if the goal is to move people away from their own choices about their welfare, it is certainly a form of paternalism. (Imagine a government that specified its preferred choices with respect to everything in life, and charged everyone one cent for each departure from those preferred choices; that government would be acting paternalistically.)

In fact it might be most sensible to understand paternalistic interventions in terms of a continuum from hardest to softest, with the points marked in accordance with the magnitude of the costs (of whatever kind) imposed on choosers by choice architects. On this view, there is no sharp distinction between hard and soft paternalism; all we have are points along a continuum. But differences of degree are important. We should agree that there is a big difference between, say, a severe criminal ban on smoking marijuana and a nominal civil fine, and between a prison sentence for failing to buckle your seatbelt and a graphic educational campaign offering vivid warnings.

Under this approach, a statement that paternalism is "hard" would mean that choice architects are imposing large costs on choosers, whereas a statement that paternalism is "soft" would mean that the costs are small. All costs, material or non-material, would count, and to assess the degree of hardness, we would inquire into their magnitude. For example, psychic costs, like those produced by graphic warnings, could move an intervention along the continuum toward hard paternalism, if those costs turned out to be high. Nudges would count as soft paternalism as long as they impose no or very small costs on choosers. If their goal is to protect people from their own mistakes, they would run afoul of the Harm Principle— but as we shall see, they might nonetheless be justified.

There are significant advantages in seeing a continuum here rather than a categorical distinction. But if a categorical distinction is what is sought, we might want to focus on whether the intervention imposes material costs. On this approach, we would understand "hard paternalism" to refer to *actions of government that attempt to improve people's welfare by imposing material costs on their choices.* By contrast, "soft paternalism" would refer to *actions of government that attempt to improve people's welfare by influencing their choices without imposing material costs on those choices.*

If the government engages in an advertising campaign designed to persuade people to exercise more than they now do, it is (on this view) engaging in soft paternalism. If the government requires employers automatically to enroll workers in health insurance plans, or requires warnings to accompany certain products, soft paternalism is involved (because workers can opt out and consumers can proceed despite the warnings). Soft paternalism is libertarian insofar as it does not impose material costs on people's choices. (Of course, requirements and material costs are imposed in these cases, and those requirements and costs deserve attention; the question I am exploring here is whether they are imposed on end users, such as workers and consumers.) We can understand soft paternalism, thus defined, as including nudges, and I will use the terms interchangeably here.

In a careful and illuminating book, one that is sharply critical of paternalism in any form, Riccardo Rebonato offers a provocative and different definition of libertarian paternalism, or nudges:

Libertarian paternalism is the set of interventions aimed at overcoming the unavoidable cognitive biases and decisional inadequacies of an individual by exploiting them in such a way as to influence her decisions (in an easily reversible manner) towards choices that she herself would make if she had at her disposal unlimited time and information, and the analytic abilities of a rational decision-maker (more precisely, of *Homo Economicus*).[9]

This definition is useful, but it is imprecise in three respects. First, the universe of nudges is far broader than the definition suggests. Soft paternalism includes interventions (such as warnings and default rules) that may be helpful but that need not specifically counteract biases and decisional inadequacies. Second, the word "counteracting" is better than "exploiting." Nudges can counteract biases (such as unrealistic optimism) without exploiting anything. Third, the words "easily reversible" are imprecise, because they could capture (for example) small civil penalties, even though they do not count as libertarian.

Emphasizing the idea of a continuum, we should recognize that approaches that impose (high) psychic costs, and thus target System 1, may have a greater effect, and thus turn out to be less soft, than approaches that impose (low) material costs. With respect to health risks, a graphic warning may be more effective than a tiny tax. Indeed, an approach that imposes psychic costs might greatly affect both beliefs and actions, and hence make all the difference to social outcomes. An emphasis on material costs may be useful for purposes of taxonomy, but such costs are hardly all that matter, and the tools that impose these costs are not necessarily the most influential ones in the paternalist's toolbox.

Here is another angle on the problem. People are often affected by the social meaning of their action. If the meaning of risk taking is bravery and leadership, people might well take risks. If the meaning of risk taking is cowardice, foolishness, and timid conformity, people will be less likely to take risks. Consider the fact that the meaning of buckling one's seatbelts has shifted dramatically over time. What was once cowardice, or an accusation directed against the driver, is now simple prudence. In many communities, the social meaning of smoking has changed as well. Social meanings are a central part of society's choice architecture, and they are often taken for granted, even though they could be otherwise. In many ways, we experience social meanings in the same way that fish experience water. Nonetheless, social meanings count as significant nudges. They impose the equivalent of subsidies and taxes. We can ignore them if we wish, but much of the time, they help to drive our thought and behavior.

Individuals cannot change social meanings on their own.[10] To alter them, it is necessary to solve a collective action problem. Laws that require people to buckle their seatbelts or that ban drunk driving do exactly that, and to the extent that they solve a collective action problem, they should not be seen as paternalistic at all. Nudges can have the same effect—as, for example, through warnings or educational campaigns designed to alter the social meaning of certain actions. Because people sometimes live in accordance with social meanings that they abhor, efforts to alter those meanings, through government, cannot be ruled off-limits. Most or all of the public might affirmatively seek the new meanings, and they might not want to be influenced or trapped by the old ones. And if their efforts at changing meanings come through nudges, the risk of government overreaching is significantly reduced.

Means and Ends

I have noted the importance of distinguishing between means paternalism and ends paternalism. In acting paternalistically, government might well accept people's ends but conclude that their choices will not promote those ends. A GPS provides information about how to get from one place to another. People can ignore what the GPS says and try their own route, but if they do, they run a risk of undermining their own ends (and people know that).

The GPS is an iconic nudge. It should be seen as a form of means paternalism, and means paternalists want to build on the GPS example. They seek to give people a sense of the best route, given their own ends. If, for example, consumers want to make a sensible trade-off between up-front costs and long-term fuel costs, but sometimes fail to do so (perhaps because long-term costs are not salient), means paternalists might take steps to steer them in the direction of considering all relevant costs at the time of purchase. We have seen that disclosure is the most natural solution, but we have also seen that means paternalists would consider a fuel-economy mandate if they were convinced that such a mandate would promote consumers' ends. The analogy here would be to a GPS that forces cars to take the best or most sensible route—to be sure, a far from entirely attractive idea (what if people enjoy certain scenery, or have a sentimental attachment to a longer route?), but perhaps appealing for some people and at some times and places. The idea of the coercive GPS can be seen as a model and a test for hard paternalism with respect to means.

Ends paternalists have far more ambitious goals. They might think, for example, that longevity is what is most important. They might insist that even if people disagree and are willing to run certain risks for reasons they believe to be good and sufficient, paternalists can legitimately steer them toward longevity. Or ends paternalists might believe that certain sexual activity is inconsistent with people's well-being, suitably defined, and hence they should not be allowed to engage in that activity. Or ends paternalism might think that people should follow certain religious practices, indeed that their salvation depends on it, and ends paternalists might seek or adopt initiatives to increase the likelihood that they will do so.

Both means paternalists and ends paternalists might run afoul of the Harm Principle, but for those who believe that people know what is in their best interests, ends paternalism is especially alarming. Mill's own discussion supports this point. He suggests that the "only freedom which deserves the name, is that of pursuing our own good in our own way, so long as we do not attempt to deprive others of theirs, or impede their efforts to obtain it. . . . Mankind are greater gainers by suffering each other to live as seems good to themselves."[11] Recall that for the most part, behavioral economists have not sought to revisit people's ends, and their findings do not support ends paternalism. They have generally emphasized human errors with respect to means, and hence means paternalism is their principal interest and also my main focus here.

Means or Ends?

While the distinction between means paternalism and ends paternalism captures something important, it raises a number of hard questions, and the line between the two is not always sharp. Some of the most straightforward cases of means paternalism involve shrouded attributes, optimistic bias, and availability bias. Suppose that people want a refrigerator that will perform well and cost as little as possible. If government ensures that people have accurate information about cost, it is not revisiting their ends in any way. It is not even acting paternalistically, in the sense that it is informing people's choices rather than (independently) influencing them. The same can be said if people underestimate the risks of distracted driving or of smoking. If the government corrects people's unrealistic optimism, or counteracts their use of the availability heuristic in order to produce an accurate judgment about probability, it is respecting their ends. We might not want to characterize this action as paternalistic at all.

So too if, for example, people are ignoring certain product attributes because those attributes are shrouded. If those attributes would matter to people who attended to them, then efforts to promote disclosure do not question people's ends. Consider, for example, the multiple disclosure requirements in the 2009 Credit Card Accountability Responsibility and Disclosure (CARD) Act, which are designed to ensure that cardholders are not surprised by late fees and overuse fees. Small nudges, informing people of the costs of such fees in advance, have contributed to annual savings, as a result of the CARD Act, of more than $20 billion.[12] Of course, it may be hard to determine whether people are in fact ignoring shrouded attributes, or whether they simply do not much care about them. But so far, at least, there is no problem of ends paternalism, and so long as only disclosure is involved,

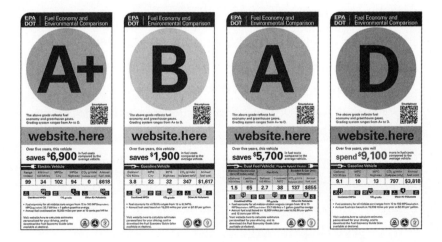

Fig. 2.1: Proposed Fuel Economy Labels
Credit: Environmental Protection Agency, Fuel Economy Label, online at
http://www.epa.gov/fueleconomy/label/nprm-label2010.pdf

there might not be paternalism at all. If efforts to alter choice architecture are more aggressive—if they involve economic incentives designed to discourage the relevant behavior, or flat bans—then they would qualify as paternalistic. Nonetheless, they would seem to count as means paternalism if they are designed only to ensure that people achieve their own ends.[13]

Even apparently easy cases, however, raise complications. Consider a fuel economy label, designed to inform people of the cost over a year or a five-year period of particular cars. Suppose that the government provides this information through a vivid letter grade—say, an "A" or a "B," as in fact was proposed (but not finalized) by the Department of Transportation and the Environmental Protection Agency (figure 2.1).[14]

In providing letter grades, the government is not merely providing people with facts. True, this is hardly the most aggressive form of paternalism about either means or ends. But formal grades go beyond a GPS. Indeed, they might be taken as a form of paternalism not merely about means but also about ends *insofar as government is singling out the particular variable of fuel economy and attempting to focus people's attention on that variable, as opposed to numerous other variables that remain ungraded.* And ultimately, the government declined to require letter grades in part on the ground that such grades might be taken, wrongly, to suggest that government was giving "all things considered" grades to cars.[15]

But I am making a different point here. Even if this risk did not exist, a fuel-economy grade could be taken as paternalistic, and to involve a degree of paternalism about ends as well as means, insofar as it would focus people's attention on one of innumerable features of cars. Government does not, after all, give serious consideration to requiring letter grades for speed, acceleration, brightness of color, stylishness, or coolness. (Compare the Simply 600 menu of The Daily Grill. We do not observe a Simply 1200 menu, or a Plenty of Salt menu, or a More Sugar, Please, menu.)

Even without letter grades, any fuel-economy label has at least a degree of paternalism, certainly about means and indeed about ends as well, insofar as it isolates fuel economy, rather than other imaginable features of cars, for compulsory

Gasoline Vehicle

Fig. 2.2: Final Fuel Economy and Environment Label
Credit: Environmental Protection Agency, Final Rule on Revisions and
Additions to Motor Vehicle Fuel Economy Label, 76 Fed. Reg. at 39480
figure I-1

display. This is so even if the label includes "just the facts."
Figure 2.2 shows the label that in 2010, the government actually chose to require.

Consider a thought experiment or perhaps a little science
fiction. We should be able to agree that government would
focus only on means, and indeed would not be paternalistic
at all, if it could have some kind of access to every person's
internal concerns and provide them with accurate information about everything that already concerns each of them.
Perhaps in the fullness of time, government or the private

sector will be able to do something like that. But insofar as government is being selective, it is at least modestly affecting people's ends, perhaps even intentionally.

Of course people want to save money; that is one of their ends. But government chose a fuel-economy label, rather than an acceleration label or a coolness label, because fuel economy was the feature of cars on which public officials sought to focus consumer attention. (It is also possible that fuel economy is more shrouded than other features, not in the sense that it is literally hidden but because and to the extent that it is not highly salient; but that is hardly self-evident.) To this we might add the more familiar point that any disclosure requirement has to be framed in a certain way, and the choice of frame may affect people's decisions and even their ends. Notice, for example, that the final fuel-economy label offers a good deal of environmental information, involving emissions of greenhouse gases and smog. The decision to emphasize that information will undoubtedly have an impact on some people's choices. If environmental factors had been given more prominence, the impact would be larger. So long as a label has a design, it is likely to influence both means and ends. In requiring that the label describe some of the environmental effects of a car's fuel economy, Congress was probably seeking to do exactly that.

It is reasonable to say that government would be focused solely on means if it provided people with accurate information about everything that they cared about and did not provide information about things that they did not care about. In that event, disclosure would not be paternalistic at all. It would be entirely means-focused, and it would not attempt to influence choices except insofar as it would promote accurate beliefs, which is not a paternalistic endeavor. But if government frames a disclosure policy with the purpose and effect not only of informing but also of influencing people's choices, it is engaging in a form of soft paternalism—under certain assumptions, about ends as well as means. And if government's disclosure policy is selective, in the sense that it requires disclosure with respect to one attribute (that people care about) but not others (that people also care about), it is again engaging in a form of soft paternalism about means and also ends— unless it can be shown that the selected attribute is, distinctly, one on which people now lack and need information.

But we really should not be too fussy or clever here, and we should avoid tying ourselves into conceptual knots. If framing or selectivity is at work, there may be a form of ends paternalism, but it is likely to be of a very modest kind, perhaps so modest that we do not have to worry much. If the characteristic is one that people antecedently do care about—like money— then it is fair to say that any paternalism is at least centrally about means, and that the intrusion on people's ends is small and possibly even incidental.

In the domain of procrastination and time inconsistency, however, the distinction between means paternalism and ends paternalism becomes more troubled still. Suppose that people do procrastinate and that they make decisions that harm their future selves. In addressing those problems, are paternalists addressing means or ends? If ends, whose? At what time?

At Time 1, the person chose to smoke, to drink, and to eat a lot; at Time 2, the (same) person wishes that she had made none of those choices.[16] To know whether a paternalistic intervention is about means or about ends, we might have to identify the level of generality at which people's ends are to be described. If the end is "for life to go well," then all forms of paternalism, including the most ambitious, seem to qualify as means paternalism, since they are styled as means to that most general and abstract of ends. But if the end is very specific— "To buy this product today!" or "To smoke this cigarette right now!"—then many and perhaps all forms of paternalism qualify as ends paternalism. If ends are described at a level of great specificity, there may be no such thing as means paternalism.

In the hard cases of procrastination and time inconsistency, the "means or ends" question may not be tractable. The best solution may be to decline to answer that question directly and instead to ask about what would increase people's aggregate welfare over time, on the theory that aggregate welfare (taking all relevant values into account) is the end that people really do care about. If an effort to overcome unjustified procrastination promotes people's welfare on balance, by making their lives go better (by their own lights), it responds to a behavioral market failure and hence is plausibly justified, at least on welfare grounds. The words "plausibly justified" are important; there are many objections, and I will get to them in due course.

Another problem is that at Time 1, people have different preferences from those that they have at Time 2, and this fact complicates the inquiry into aggregate welfare. And of course public officials face formidable conceptual and empirical problems in deciding what promotes aggregate welfare over time[17]—a point that argues in favor of soft rather than hard paternalism, and one to which I will return.

A Quick Summary

Summarizing these various points, we can imagine the following possibilities, with illustrative examples (table 2.1). Where behavioral market failures justify corrective action, the government should be inclined to stay in the upper-left

Table 2.1   Types of Paternalism

	Means Paternalism	Ends Paternalism
Soft Paternalism	Fuel-economy labels	Automatic enrollment in particular religion or political party (with opt-out provision)
Hard Paternalism	Fuel-economy standards	Criminal ban on same-sex relations

quadrant, unless strong empirical justifications, involving relevant costs and benefits, support a more aggressive approach. Recall the First Law of Behaviorally Informed Regulation, which is that in the face of behavioral market failures, nudges are generally the right response. Moreover, those who emphasize behavioral market failures would seek to avoid both quadrants on the right-hand side.

ON WELFARE

My account of paternalism raises a fundamental question. What counts as people's welfare? Does it mean happiness, narrowly conceived? Are we speaking of "utility" as Mill understood it? Shouldn't welfare include whatever makes lives good and meaningful, even if happiness, strictly speaking, is not involved? For now, and to keep the focus on the issue of paternalism, I am going to understand the term "welfare" very broadly. Under that broad understanding, the capacious idea of welfare can be separated from the narrower one of utility, and it can include many elements of life that may not count as "happiness." Mill himself spoke of "utility in the largest sense, grounded on the progressive interests of man as a progressive being,"[18] and this conception of utility is not purely hedonic; it includes many goods others than moment-by-moment happiness. We could imagine more capacious understandings as well, including values that people hold that are not necessarily "grounded on the progressive interests of man as a progressive being." We should also notice the importance of distinguishing between "welfare" from the standpoint of the chooser and "welfare" from the standpoint of the paternalist.

With respect to the chooser, let us understand the term to refer to whatever choosers think would make their lives go well.[19] Mill himself suggested a difference between higher and lower pleasures, and urged that the distinction could be justified by reference to the views of choosers themselves:

> If I am asked what I mean by difference of quality in pleasures, or what makes one pleasure more valuable than another, merely as a pleasure, except its being greater in amount, there is but one possible answer. Of two pleasures, if there be one to which all or almost all who have experience of both give a decided preference, irrespective of any feeling of moral obligation to prefer it, that is the more desirable pleasure. If one of the two is, by those who are competently acquainted with both, placed so far above the other that they prefer it, even though knowing it to be attended with a greater amount of discontent, and would not resign it for any quantity of the other pleasure which their nature is capable of, we are justified in ascribing to the preferred enjoyment a superiority

in quality so far outweighing quantity as to render it, in comparison, of small account.[20]

Perhaps Mill is right, but we could imagine many other conceptions of welfare. People's principal concerns might be religious; they might believe that fidelity to God's will is what is necessary to make their lives go well. When they think about their own lives, they may want to make choices that benefit other people—not only their friends and families, but strangers as well. They may be altruistic and believe that for their lives to go well, they must help others. They may want their lives to be meaningful, not merely full of pleasure, and they might sacrifice material and other benefits to achieve that goal. Perhaps they care a great deal about the accumulation of wealth, but perhaps not. They strike their own balance; different people will choose differently. They may or may not enjoy exercising or smoking. They may or may not care a lot about health benefits or aesthetics.

Choosers might care about the taste, amount, and nutritional content of food and drink. They might be happy to eat a lot of high-calorie foods, every day, simply because they enjoy them so much. (They might dislike or even hate calorie labels, on the ground that they detract from the enjoyment.) Or they might care not only about the economic benefits of fuel-efficient cars but also about the environment.

With respect to the paternalist, we can understand "welfare" in the same way, to refer capaciously to whatever the paternalist thinks would make choosers' lives go well. The paternalist might believe that choosers have the right ends, but that some kind of action is needed to ensure that they actually achieve those ends (perhaps because of the operation of System 1). Alternatively, the paternalist might believe that choosers have the wrong ends—perhaps the choosers do not focus enough on health, or sexual abstinence, or on what makes life meaningful, or on obedience to God's will. If so, the paternalist might believe that some kind of response is needed, with respect to actions or beliefs, to ensure that the right ends are achieved. Though paternalists might have any number of views about what would make people's lives go well, recall that I am interested in defending paternalists who respect choosers' own views about their ends, and who seek to increase the likelihood that their decisions will promote those ends.[21]

WAS MAYOR BLOOMBERG A NANNY?

New York Mayor Michael Bloomberg long sought to address a wide range of public health problems, including those associated with obesity and smoking. A number of his initiatives seem to have been behaviorally informed. Like many experts, he believes that soda is a contributing factor to increasing obesity rates and that large portion sizes are making the problem worse. In 2012, he proposed to ban the sale of sweetened drinks in containers larger than sixteen ounces at restaurants, delis, theaters, stadiums, and food courts. The New York City Board of Health approved the ban, though it was later struck down in court.

The ban does have an unmistakable behavioral logic. People tend to eat or drink whatever is put in front of them,[22] and large portion sizes contribute to obesity. If the goal is to decrease the health risks associated with obesity, smaller portion sizes are a reasonable idea. Nonetheless, many people were outraged by what they saw as an egregious illustration of the nanny state in action. Why shouldn't people be allowed to choose a large bottle of Coca-Cola, if that's what they want? The Center for Consumer Freedom responded with a vivid advertisement, depicting Mayor Bloomberg in a (scary) nanny outfit (figure 2.3).

But self-interested industries were not the only source of ridicule. Jon Stewart is a comedian, but he was hardly amused. A representative remark from one of his commentaries: "No! . . . I love this idea you have of banning sodas larger than 16 ounces. It combines the draconian government overreach people love with the probable lack of results they expect."

Was the proposed Big Gulp ban hard or soft? Did it involve means or ends? Neither question is easy to answer. We should be able to agree that the ban would not have been a mere nudge. Because it would have precluded people from purchasing sodas in large containers, it would not retain free-

Fig. 2.3: The Nanny
Credit: The Center for Consumer Freedom

dom of choice. On the other hand, it would hardly have been an aggressive form of paternalism. If people wanted to drink a lot of ounces of soda, they could certainly do that, simply by purchasing several containers. If we see a continuum from soft to hard paternalism, the Big Gulp initiative was relatively soft.

A plausible defense of the initiative would insist that it attempted to promote people's ends, not to overrule them. People want to be healthy, and by reducing the risk of obesity, the initiative would do exactly that. Hardly anyone wants to be obese. But for reasons that we have explored, this argument is too simple. People's ends are not limited to health. They want to consume the drinks that they enjoy, in the sizes that they prefer. For choosers who sought soda in large containers, the ban would affect their ends, not simply their means to those ends.

What emerges is that Mayor Bloomberg ventured a relatively soft form of nonlibertarian paternalism, one that could not be defended as merely affecting people's means. Was his initiative defensible? In brief, the answer should turn on its costs and benefits. Its costs appear real but low, both to choosers and to providers. With respect to benefits, the question is whether it would have a significant impact on the obesity problem—a question on which we appear to lack much data. For these reasons, it is not obvious whether the initiative was a good one, and strong views either way are not easy to defend.

Let us compare another behaviorally informed initiative from Mayor Bloomberg, one that would prohibit the display of cigarettes in most retail shops. Under this approach, cigarettes could certainly be sold, but they would no longer be visible or salient to consumers. Here as well, the initiative has an unmistakable behavioral logic. As we have seen, salience greatly matters to people's choices. But unlike the Big Gulp ban, this approach is not merely a form of soft paternalism but also a genuine nudge, enlisting choice architecture on behalf of public health.

Mayor Bloomberg's approach here is not unlike that of Google, which found that its New York cafeteria, which offered a lot of high-calorie items, was producing a lot of unwanted pounds. In response to employee complaints, the company initiated a series of changes to nudge people toward more healthful choices. Large plates and takeout containers were exchanged for smaller sizes, and employees were encouraged to eat less with a sign stating, "People who take big plates tend to eat more." The redesigned cafeteria took a number of smart steps to make healthful choices simpler and more convenient (and to make less healthful choices less so). As a result, it helped to produce real reductions in both calories and fat consumed from candy. Google created a kind of Nudge Cafeteria, designed to increase healthful choices. Mayor Bloomberg took a broadly similar approach for cigarettes.

At the same time, it must be agreed that the prohibition on open display could affect ends as well as means, because purchasing cigarettes is, for some, a genuine end (at least if we are describing ends at a level of specificity). And in this case, as in that of the Big Gulp ban, the overall assessment should turn on both costs and benefits. That assessment would require a great deal of information about likely effects. But in view of the serious adverse health effects of smoking, and its addictive character, it is certainly plausible to think that this is an excellent nudge.

HARM TO OTHERS

Consistent with the Harm Principle, my working definition of paternalism does not include government efforts to prevent people from harming others—as, for example, in the case of assault or theft, or air pollution. There is nothing paternalistic about preventing people from beating you up, stealing your car, or making the air hazardous for you to breathe. Nor does the definition include government efforts to promote certain familiar and widely held social goals; consider laws designed to protect privacy, to protect endangered species, or to prevent discrimination on the basis of race, sex, religion, disability, and sexual orientation. None of these is fundamentally rooted in paternalistic considerations.[23] By contrast, the definition does include government efforts to override or influence people's judgments about whether it is best for them to worship a particular God, to drink alcohol, to gamble, to drive while talking on their cell phones, or to eat a dozen peanut butter cookies before, during, or after dinner.

True, and important, some of the latter cases might turn out to involve harm to others. If you drive while talking on your cell phone, you might well endanger other people, and a restriction could be defended for that reason. If you are making yourself drunk or even sick, you might affect others. In the cases just described, it is possible that regulation can be justified on grounds that have nothing to do with paternalism. To see some of the complexities here, recall recent rules that require increases in fuel economy. We have seen that such rules produce substantial social benefits by reducing air pollution and by increasing energy security; producing these benefits does not involve paternalism. But as we have also seen, the strong majority of the benefits of such rules come from private fuel savings, and producing those benefits might reasonably be thought to involve paternalism. To get clear on the underlying issues, and to keep the focus on paternalism, let us put third-party effects entirely to one side.

If we begin with this definition, the central objection to paternalistic interventions, elaborated most famously by Mill, is that people should be free to choose as they see fit. We should be able to see that while the principal objection is to ends paternalism, means paternalism runs into serious concerns as well. Even in the face of behavioral market failures, why should public officials be authorized to interfere with people's judgments about the best means to promote their ends? Mightn't officials err as well, and possibly more damagingly? These are important questions, but one of my principal goals here is to suggest that insofar as Mill's view neglects the existence of behavioral market failures, and the wide range of behavioral findings about human errors, it points in the wrong directions.[24]

The Paternalist's Large Toolbox

To know whether and what kind of paternalism is involved, and to get clearer on the underlying concepts, we need to be more specific about the set of tools that government might use. Consider some possibilities:

1. Government says that no one may smoke cigarettes and that the sanction for smoking cigarettes is a criminal penalty—of $500.

2. Government says that no one may smoke cigarettes and that the sanction for smoking cigarettes is a criminal penalty—of $0.01.

3. Government says that no one may smoke cigarettes and that the sanction for smoking cigarettes is a civil fine—of $500.

4. Government says that no one may smoke cigarettes and that the sanction for smoking is a civil fine—of $0.01.

5. Government does not say that no one may smoke cigarettes, but instead imposes a tax on cigarette purchases—a tax of $3.00 per pack.

6. Government does not say that no one may smoke cigarettes, but creates a program to help smokers to quit, including a "quit line" offering access to people who are experts in promoting smoking cessation.

7. Government does not say that no one may smoke cigarettes, but creates a program that provides a financial subsidy to smokers who quit for six months—a subsidy of $500.

8. Government does not say that no one may smoke cigarettes, but instead engages in a vivid, frightening advertising campaign, emphasizing the dangers of smoking.[25]

9. Government does not say that no one may smoke cigarettes, but instead requires packages to contain vivid, frightening images, emphasizing the dangers of smoking.[26]

10. Government does not say that no one may smoke cigarettes, but instead engages in a public education campaign designed to make smoking seem deviant, or antisocial, or uncool.

11. Government does not say that no one may smoke cigarettes, but instead engages in a truthful, fact-filled educational campaign disclosing the dangers of smoking.

12. Government does not say that no one may smoke cigarettes, but instead requires packages to provide truthful information disclosing the dangers of smoking.

13. Government does not say that no one may smoke cigarettes, but instead requires cigarette sellers to place cigarettes in an inconspicuous place, so that people will not happen across them and must affirmatively ask for them. (Recall Mayor Bloomberg's initiative.)

14. Government does not say that no one may smoke cigarettes, but instead requires cigarettes to be sold in small con-

tainers, each having no more than eight cigarettes. (Cigarette packs usually have twenty cigarettes now.)

Those who begin with the definition I have offered should acknowledge that all of these cases are not the same. If we are focused on leaving freedom of choice unaffected by government, and use the definition offered above, approaches (1) through (5), involving penalties, would count as forms of paternalism, even though approaches (2) and (4) count as soft, because the penalty is so low. Approaches (6) and (7) might seem more difficult to categorize. Is it paternalistic to promote efforts to cease engaging in certain action? Does paternalism include not merely penalties but also subsidies? What about selective subsidies, as in, for example, a decision to allow recipients to use food stamps to pay for almost all food and drink, but not soda or chocolate bars? (In 2011, Mayor Bloomberg asked the United States Department of Agriculture for permission not to allow food stamps to be used to pay for soda; the Department denied the petition.)[27] Insofar as a cessation program or a subsidy is designed to influence a person's choices on the ground that those choices would not promote his or her welfare, it should be counted as paternalistic (even if some people do not object to those forms of paternalism).

By contrast, disclosure of truthful information is not ordinarily understood as paternalistic. As we have seen, the basic reason is that disclosure requirements are meant to inform, not to displace, people's understanding of which choices will promote their welfare. But we have also seen several complexities here. First, disclosure of information will often affect that understanding, especially to the extent that it is selective. Second, the framing of information matters,[28] and any disclosure requirement will inevitably include a certain kind of framing. It may be disputed whether a given disclosure requirement is simply informing choices; some forms of disclosure can certainly fall within the category of soft paternalism.

What about approaches (8) and (9), involving the use of vivid, frightening images? I have emphasized that psychic costs, no less than material costs, can alter behavior; indeed, psychic costs might have the same effect as large material ones. Some people might think that efforts to frighten people, and thus to go beyond mere disclosure of facts and to grab the attention of System 1, can be taken as a form of (soft) paternalism. Under the definition I have offered, it is more than plausible to hold this view. Indeed, at least one court has drawn a distinction of this kind for First Amendment purposes, suggesting that compelled disclosure of facts is different from, and more acceptable than, compelled graphic warnings.[29] As a matter of First Amendment law, I do not agree with that position, but it is true that efforts to stigmatize a product or an activity, and to do so through emotional appeals, impose a psychic or affective cost on purchase or use. Imposition of affective costs is paralleled by the creation of affective benefits, which could come, for example, by efforts to portray certain activities, such as exercising or eating vegetables, in a positive light; such approaches could also be characterized as soft paternalism.

Approaches (13) and (14) also involve forms of soft paternalism. If officials put a product in an inconspicuous place, and if their goal is to discourage its purchase, they are steering people in a certain direction because they distrust people's own judgments about what would promote their welfare. No monetary penalty is involved, but time and effort must be expended to find the relevant goods. And if government requires a product to be sold in small containers so that people will consume less of it, it is behaving paternalistically insofar as it is making it harder for them to make the choices that they prefer. True, choice architecture is inevitable. True, many people may prefer that private or public institutions impose such costs, and some or many smokers may themselves share that preference, because they would like to quit. But the point remains.

Paternalism and Welfare

By itself, an understanding of human error cannot justify paternalism. We need to have a sense of what paternalism is *for*—of what it would actually achieve in people's lives. The obvious answer is that if choice architects are armed with an understanding of where people go wrong, they are in a good position to help people go right. The central idea is that some forms of paternalism can enable people to have better lives (by their own lights). If there is a moral argument on behalf of paternalism, this is where it resides.

Because we are focusing here on paternalism from the government, we should observe that if welfare is our guide, there are special concerns in that context. Many people think that it is not unacceptable if a private employer acts paternalistically in an effort to protect its employees, or if a credit card company does so in an effort to protect its customers, or if a restaurant acts to promote healthy eating. Because of the operation of the free market, harmful, insulting, or unjustified paternalism will ultimately be punished. (As noted, this is unrealistic in some cases.)[1] But if government acts paternalistically—to improve health, to lengthen lives, to save money—many people believe that the risks are far more serious and altogether different. Certainly it is true that many of the most prominent objections to paternalist interventions (decrying "elitism," "government overreach," or "the nanny state") have a great deal to do with the distinctive social role of particular paternalists: those who work for the government.

Many of the concerns about paternalistic government focus on the idea of "legitimacy," but in this context, at least, it is possible that the idea is a placeholder, or question-begging, or perhaps even a mystification, rather than a freestanding concept. True, it might qualify as freestanding insofar as government action is challenged as insufficiently democratic, but I am assuming that we are dealing with democratic government and hence that there is no such objection here. The real question is whether the action at issue makes people's lives better or intrudes on their autonomy.

Some people ask, "How can public officials legitimately interfere with the free choices of adults?" The question is not a bad start, but it should not be taken as rhetorical. On the contrary, it is less than helpful, because the abstract question of legitimacy mostly confuses matters. It diverts attention from what really matters: people's lives.

People might really enjoy running, spending, sleeping, having sex, singing, jumping, smoking, drinking, gambling, or (over)eating. They might have their own views about how, exactly, to go about enjoying those activities. Thus Mill writes that "the strongest of all arguments against the interference of the public with purely personal conduct is that when it does interfere, the odds are that it interferes wrongly, and in the wrong place."[2] Mill also notes that we can easily "imagine an ideal public, which leaves the freedom and choice of individuals in all uncertain matters undisturbed, and only requires them to abstain from modes of conduct which universal experience has condemned. But where has there been seen a public which set any such limits to its censorship? Or when does the public trouble itself about universal experience?"

One of the major objections to paternalism, in all its forms, builds directly on these concerns. It relies, of course, on the Epistemic Argument, but it has a number of other arrows in its quiver. My purpose in this chapter is to explore the welfarist objection to paternalism. We shall see that while the argument has a great deal of force, it cannot be accepted in the abstract. In many areas, it points in exactly the wrong directions.

Everyone should agree that there are political constraints on the actions of a paternalistic government, at least in a democratic society. On an optimistic view, those constraints will sharply limit the occasions for harmful or unjustified paternalism. If public officials engage in stupid or damaging acts of paternalism, they will face electoral retribution, and the prospect of retribution will deter them from undertaking such acts. But this expectation is too optimistic, especially in view of the fact that some forms of paternalism are not salient or highly visible, and the associated fact that well-organized private groups, with their own interests at stake, may wish to move public policy in their preferred directions, and endorse paternalism for that reason. Political accountability is important, even crucial, but it is hardly a complete safeguard against ill-motivated or harmful paternalism.

I focus on welfarist concerns in this chapter and turn to autonomy in the next. I begin with a set of apparently powerful welfarist objections to paternalism and then turn to responses, focusing on the fact that as an empirical matter, paternalism can in fact increase people's welfare. I suggest that a great deal depends on context and that the objections cannot be shown to be convincing in the abstract. Those objections operate at too high a level of generality, potentially making them into a form of chest-thumping.

Five Welfarist Objections: An Antipaternalist's Quintet

THE EPISTEMIC ARGUMENT, SPECIFIED

Suppose that we care about people's welfare, understood broadly to capture how well their lives are going. Suppose that we believe that people's lives should go as well as possible. With Mill, we might insist that individuals know best about what will make their lives go well and that public officials are likely to err. Such officials might be mistaken about what people's ends are; they might also be mistaken about the best means of achieving those ends. Most important, individuals know their own situations, and they know what they value and like, and they are likely to know how to get what they value and like. By contrast, officials have merely general or abstract information, which will not be enough. With respect to the welfare of an individual, general information will almost inevitably be inferior to the information held by that individual.

We have seen that the distinction between means and ends is a troubled one. Paternalists might see certain activities as mere means, but they might actually be ends. People might enjoy a fattening meal or a spending spree for its own sake, not because it is a means to something else. System 1 helps to establish a lot of our ends, and choice architects might miss this fact, wrongly judging choosers as selecting the wrong means.

The Epistemic Argument insists that so long as they are not harming others, people should be allowed to act on the basis of their own judgments, because those judgments are the best guide to what will make their lives go well. The central objection, applicable to any kind of paternalism (soft or hard, means or ends), is that errors are more likely to come from officials than from individuals. Public officials lack the information that individuals have.

COMPETITION

In a free economy, companies compete with one another, and people are free to choose among a wide range of options. If cars have poor fuel economy and end up costing a lot over time, companies will compete to improve fuel economy. If a refrigerator is not cold enough and if it costs a lot of money to operate, it will not do well in the market. Companies will produce better refrigerators that cost less. If important features of products are shrouded and turn out to be bad, they will eventually be revealed, and companies will no longer be able to shroud them. If people are optimistic, and if credit card companies exploit their unrealistic optimism, people will find out and seek other providers. Some consumers can be fooled or tricked, but in the long run, the process of competition will help a great deal.

We have seen that participants in the market might be able

to counteract all of the problems identified here. Companies themselves can help promote self-control on the part of their customers. They can reveal shrouded attributes. They can counteract unrealistic optimism. They can promote an accurate understanding of probability. They might even specialize in correcting behavioral market failures (perhaps making the very category disappear). As technologies evolve, such correctives are increasingly available. For every behavioral market failure, it may soon be possible to say, with the old Apple commercial, "There's an app for that."

It is a major problem if paternalistic approaches end up freezing the process of competition. Especially if such approaches are hard rather than soft, they may impair the operation of a competitive process that produces a mixture of diverse products that are well-suited to diverse tastes and circumstances. In his greatest and most enduring contribution to social theory, Friedrich Hayek emphasized the dispersed nature of human knowledge and the informational advantages of markets, incorporating that dispersed knowledge, over even the most intelligent and well-motivated planners.[3] We can thus identify a Hayekian challenge to paternalism. Even if public officials are armed with knowledge of behavioral market failures, and even if they are public-spirited, they will do far worse than free markets, which can produce a wide range of products and rapid responses to changing tastes and needs. Especially if it is rigid, paternalism may well have a range of unintended consequences, many of them quite bad, and those consequences may not be predicted or foreseen by even the wisest and most benign choice architects.

LEARNING

It is true that people err and that their errors can impair their welfare. But mistakes are often productive. Life is a movie, not a snapshot, and people can learn from what goes wrong. We should not freeze people's frames. On one view, government ought not to short-circuit the valuable process of learning-by-doing. That process greatly increases human welfare. Indeed, people develop preferences and values and become better choosers as a result. If people make mistakes about diets, drinks, love, or investments, they can obtain valuable lessons, and those lessons can make their lives go much better. A paternalistic government infantilizes people; it treats them like children and makes it less likely that they will grow up. Mill made a related point, emphasizing that "the free development of individuality is one of the leading essentials of well-being" and indeed that "it is not only a coordinate element with all that is designated by the terms civilization, instruction, education, culture, but is itself a necessary part and condition of all those things."[4]

Perhaps there is no reasonable concern about efforts to ensure that people's choices are well informed—at least if those efforts do not discourage people from learning on their own. But if people are defaulted into a particular savings or health care plan, rather than being asked to choose such a plan for themselves, learning is less likely to occur. Hard paternalism is worse, but soft paternalism can also infantilize citizens by reducing such learning (and liberty in the process).

For those who emphasize the value of learning, it might seem best for choice architects to call for *active choosing* rather than default rules.[5] In many areas, government might dispense with default rules and instead require people to make choices on their own. For savings plans, health insurance, organ donation, and much more, choice architects might insist that people have to say what they want. Perhaps this approach can itself be counted as a form of soft paternalism insofar as it steers people toward active choosing, when people have not made an active choice in favor of active choosing. Those who prefer active choosing are not avoiding nudges; they are nudging. They are not avoiding libertarian paternalism; they are engaging in it.

But even if this is so, active choosing will be found congenial to those who emphasize both learning and liberty. Thus Mill noted that conformity to custom "does not educate or develop ... any of the qualities which are the distinctive endowment of a human being. The human faculties of perception, judgment, discriminative feeling, mental activity, are exercised only in making a choice. . . . The mental and moral, like the muscular powers, are improved only by being used."[6] A default rule is not precisely custom as Mill understood it, but his fear of the "despotism of custom," as "the standing hindrance of human advancement," is far from irrelevant.[7]

Human populations are highly diverse in terms of tastes and values, and many different kinds of lives can be good. Mill himself was emphatic on this point, objecting that the "practical principle which guides" people "in their opinions on the regulation of human conduct, is the feeling in each person's mind that everybody should be required to act as he, and those with whom he sympathizes, would like them to act. No one, indeed, acknowledges to himself that his standard of judgment is his own liking."[8] And in a famous passage, emphasizing the value of diversity and experiments, Mill urged that "[a]s it is useful that while mankind are imperfect there should be different opinions, so is it that there should be different experiments of living; that free scope should be given to varieties of character, short of injury to others; and that the world of different modes of life should be proved practically, when any one thinks fit to try them. It is desirable, in short, that in things which do not primarily concern others, individuality should assert itself."[9]

For paternalists, the problem is that one size is unlikely to fit all. With respect to diet, savings, exercise, romance, credit cards, mortgages, cell phones, health care, computers, and much more, different people have divergent tastes and situations, and they balance the relevant values in different ways.[10] In many contexts, an effort to impose a single size will reduce people's welfare on balance.

The same is true with respect to trade-offs between the present and the future. People have diverse ends and they choose diverse means. Young people make different trade-offs from those made by old people. It is hardly irrational to value the present more than the future, and different discount rates can reasonably be chosen by people who are in different life circumstances. There may be no self-control problem if people decide to enjoy today and tomorrow, even if the consequence is not ideal for the day after. As Mill wrote, "it is a privilege and proper condition of a human being, arrived at the maturity of his faculties, to use and interpret experience in his own way. It is for him to find out what part of recorded experience is properly applicable to his own circumstances and character."[11]

To be sure, we should not rely on abstractions here. We have to investigate the details, and relevant empirical questions, to know whether and how heterogeneity matters. If people are required to buckle their seatbelts or to wear motorcycle helmets, and if they are forbidden to text while driving, it is at least imaginable that no matter how diverse the population, the welfare of the overwhelming majority will be increased as a result. On plausible assumptions, they will live longer and safer lives, and they will not lose a lot.

The admittedly serious problems with one-size-fits-all approaches should not be taken to suggest that one size never fits all. With respect to one-size-fits-all approaches, universal skepticism is itself a one-size-fits-all approach, and a bad one. But the simple fact of human diversity suggests that if government prescribes a certain outcome, and departs from people's own sense of what is best, human welfare might be reduced rather than increased. For those who find these points convincing, soft paternalism has significant advantages, because it ultimately allows people to go their own way. But insofar as it steers all people in the same direction, it raises problems of its own. Mill once more: "The same mode of life is a healthy excitement to one, keeping all his faculties and enjoyment in their best order, while to another it is a distracting burden, which suspends or crushes all internal life. Such are the differences among human beings in their sources of pleasure, their susceptibilities of pain, and the operation on them of different physical and moral agencies, that unless there is a corresponding diversity in their modes of life, they neither obtain their fair share of happiness, nor grow up to the mental, moral, and aesthetic stature of which their nature is capable."[12]

We should emphasize, however, that paternalists, both hard and soft, might be able to respond to the fact of heterogeneity by avoiding one-size-fits-all approaches and by attempting more personalized approaches. *Personalized paternalism* is likely to become increasingly feasible over time.[13] We can imagine highly personalized default rules, attempting to specify diverse rules for people in different circumstances. For savings plans, health insurance, and more, such approaches might draw on available information about people's own past choices or about which approach best suits different groups of people, and potentially each person, in the population. Personalized default rules might be based on demographics; a default savings plan for someone who is thirty would be different from a default savings plan for someone who is sixty. Alternatively, personalized default rules could be very narrowly targeted and perhaps even specific to each of us. If enough information is available about someone's past choices or personal situation, we could design, for that person, default rules with respect to savings, health insurance, privacy, rental car agreements, computer settings, and everything else.

Personalized default rules would reduce the problems posed by one-size-fits-all approaches, and in principle at least, personalized approaches might even eliminate those problems. To be sure, the design of personalized paternalism raises serious technical challenges, and it remains unclear whether it could fully respect heterogeneity, especially in light of the fact that people's preferences and situations change over time. There are also serious questions about personal privacy. In many ways, personalization does appear to be the wave of the future, but if continuing learning really matters, there remains a serious argument for active choosing.

It should not be necessary to emphasize that public officials have their own biases and their own motivations. With respect to efforts to defend paternalism, this point raises two separate problems. The first involves public choice theory: The judgments of officials about welfare may be influenced by the interests of powerful private groups.[14] No one can deny that at some times and places, official judgments have been distorted because of the power of such groups. The second problem is that even if they are well motivated, officials are human too, and there is no reason to think that they are immune from the kinds of biases that affect ordinary people.[15]

We can go further. The field of "behavioral public choice theory" is in its early stages, and it will develop over time. Behavioral public choice theory should supplement the standard accounts by exploring the extent to which public officials go wrong because they make the same errors that I have emphasized here.[16] True, and important, we should expect System 2 to have a great deal of authority in government, simply because government has in its employ many people whose business it is to calculate the consequences of alternative courses of action, and thus to affirm the primacy of System 2.[17] A large virtue of technocrats in government—specialists in science, economics, and law—is that they can help overcome some of the errors that might otherwise influence public as well as private judgments.[18] Recall that people cease making certain errors when they answer questions in a foreign language. Cost-benefit analysis is a foreign language, and for policymakers, it is a pretty good one, much strengthening the role of System 2.

Nonetheless, System 1 is hardly irrelevant in the public domain. There is no question that availability bias can play a role in public arenas.[19] Recent unfortunate events might lead people to think that a problem is more serious than it actually is, and the absence of such events might lead people to neglect real problems because no misfortunate comes to mind. Officials are hardly immune from availability bias: If a bad outcome has occurred in the recent past, it is highly salient, and it may affect ultimate decisions. Indeed, officials are subject to a kind of *anticipatory availability bias:* their anticipation of a terrible outcome, and of being blamed for such an outcome, can affect their judgments. Self-interested private groups aggravate the problem by repeatedly drawing official attention to bad outcomes, or promote complacency by repeatedly drawing official attention to the absence of bad outcomes. Consider, for example, the long period in which tobacco companies drew attention to longtime smokers who did not experience health problems, or current efforts by certain companies to suggest that climate change is not occurring or that if it is occurring, it is essentially benign.

Behavioral public choice theory is beginning to explore these problems in great detail. On the basis of the discussion thus far, we should be able to identify its central claims. For every bias identified for individuals, there is an accompanying bias in the public sphere. This point offers serious cautionary notes about paternalism, whether it addresses people's means or ends.

If these points are put together, the central problem with paternalism is that it will, in the end, make people's lives go worse. Because it allows for greater flexibility, soft paternalism is less objectionable than hard paternalism, but all of the foregoing points might be brought to bear against paternalism of any kind.

Welfare Revisited

These arguments are more than plausible, but we should begin by acknowledging that to some people, the arguments just sketched will fall on deaf ears. They will seem puzzling, question-begging, even perverse.

If we focus on welfare, we have to return to the initial question, which is what it means for lives to go well. Mill was both an individualist and a utilitarian, and he focused on increasing people's utility and on allowing them to go their own way. If that is our focus, and if we understand utility in a certain way, the arguments just given might well draw us directly to the Harm Principle (subject to serious empirical challenges, which should by now be evident and which are taken up in more detail below). Thus Mill urged that people ought to ask themselves, "What do I prefer?" or, "What would suit my character and disposition?" or, "What would allow the best and highest in me to have fair play, and enable it to grow and thrive?"[20] But if we have a different understanding, and if we believe that in order to go well, lives must take a particular form, the objections to paternalism will seem badly confused and perhaps unintelligible. Indeed, ends paternalism, no less than means paternalism, will seem legitimate, and not much undermined by the antipaternalist arguments made thus far.

Suppose, for example, that we are not focused on utility and that we start with a theological view that emphasizes obedience to God's commands and that does not put a high premium on freedom of choice. If so, what some people deplore as paternalism will seem to others the natural and appropriate way to ensure that people's lives go well. In a highly illuminating book, Jonathan Haidt emphasizes the existence of plural and diverse foundations for people's moral commitments.[21] The antipaternalist view depends on accepting some of those commitments and rejecting others.

To be more specific: For those who begin with a commitment to *purity*, the welfarist objections will have little force.

Suppose we think that for a life to be pure and therefore good, people must refrain from engaging in certain activities, including gambling, smoking, drinking, and overeating, and that other activities, such as sex, should occur only subject to certain restrictions. If a life goes well if and only if it is pure (in the relevant sense), then hard paternalism might seem the right course, and the antipaternalist arguments will face an obvious (and devastating) problem.

For those arguments to get off the ground, we have to start with what some will find contentious views, to the effect that human lives can go well in many different ways, and that people are generally the best judges of how to make their own lives go well. That (broadly Millian) perspective will in turn help fuel the belief that individuals are usually the best judges of what it means for their lives to go well.[22] In my view, there is a great deal to be said for that belief (subject to empirical reservations), but it must be acknowledged that many others are doubtful.

MANY CHOICES ARE ALREADY MADE FOR US

There is an independent point. The welfarist objections neglect the extent to which countless decisions are already made for us by both public and private institutions. Most of us do not decide how to make a car safe, or where to put stop signs, or how and whether to test foods to reduce the risk of disease, or whether and which antibiotics should be allowed on the market, or how to build airplanes and railroads. If we had to make all of the choices that affect us, we would be immediately overwhelmed, and our welfare would be decreased as a result. People make only a very small fraction of the decisions that actually affect them. In important cases, and for good reasons, we can opt out in various ways, but we are on a specific track if we do nothing at all.

True, we can participate in free markets, and we can also vote. For these reasons, we do have some degree of control over many of the underlying choices, as least if "we" are taken in the aggregate. But for each of us, the degree of control is modest at best. I will return to this point in more detail in chapter 4.

CHOOSING THE WRONG MEANS: THE BRIDGE EXCEPTION

Let us put the deepest issues to one side and simply notice that even if we are concerned about welfare, and even if we are inclined to think that individuals are generally the best judges of how to make their own lives go well, the word "generally" is important. With that qualification, we can see that the objections to paternalism depend on some empirical judgments. Those judgments might be wrong—not (on the behaviorally informed view I am exploring) because it is important or desirable to revise or revisit people's ends, but because and when people select the wrong means to promote their own ends.

The distinction is an uneasy one, to be sure, but at least in some cases, it is clear enough. Mill himself pointed the way in a famous passage: "If anyone saw a person attempting to cross a bridge which had been ascertained to be unsafe, and there were no time to warn him of his danger, they might seize him and turn him back without any real infringement of his liberty; for liberty consists in doing what one desires, and he does not desire to fall into the river."[23] Let us call this the Bridge Exception. We can understand it narrowly or broadly.

If we take Mill's example literally, the exception is quite narrow. It applies when three conditions are met. First, the paternalist knows, in fact, that the bridge is unsafe ("ascertained to be unsafe"); there is no doubt about that question. Second, time is of the essence and hence a warning will not work ("and there were no time to warn him of his danger"). Third, the act of paternalism ensures that its object gets what he wants ("he does not desire to fall into the river"). Thus Mill qualifies his own exception: "Nevertheless, when there is not a certainty, but only a danger of mischief, no one but the person himself can judge of the sufficiency of the motive which may prompt him to incur the risk: in this case, therefore, (unless he is a child, or delirious, or in some state of excitement or absorption incompatible with the full use of the reflecting faculty) he ought, I conceive, to be only warned of the danger; not forcibly prevented from exposing himself to it."

But we could easily understand the Bridge Exception a bit more broadly. Notice first that Mill would clearly license warnings, even though they have a paternalistic dimension, and even though they might well influence choices. The more general question is whether we might be willing to relax the second condition, at least when the first and third are met. Suppose that the choice architect knows, with certainty, that some form of paternalism (even a hard form) will ensure that the chooser ends up with what he wants. Should we really insist that time must be of the essence? Perhaps so, if we think that the choice architect is fallible, so that a warning will provide the benefits of hard paternalism without the costs. But what if we know that a warning will have lower benefits and higher costs? The case of fuel economy is highly relevant here. Under certain assumptions, fuel economy requirements give people what they really want—but fail to choose.

Of Choices and Experiences

The largest question, raised by the Bridge Exception, is this: Do people's choices in fact promote their welfare (as they themselves understand it)? The answer is knowable, at least in principle, and it is being tested, with mixed results. We learn more every day. The findings discussed in chapter 1 suggest that behavioral market failures are far from uncommon, and as we have seen, they supplement the standard (welfarist) justifications for government action. If people pay too little attention to the long term, and enjoy short-term benefits at the expense of significant long-term costs, then a concern for people's welfare might require, rather than forbid, certain forms of paternalism (potentially including hard forms). If people procrastinate, and if System 1 is the reason, then their failure to alter the status quo may be a mistake, with possibly bad and even dangerous consequences.

To avoid misunderstanding: The point here is emphatically not that System 2 should be in charge and that what appeals to System 1 does not much matter. There is no claim that life must be dry, chocolate-free, and long. The point is instead that people make mistakes about what they would enjoy—or to return to our terms, that System 1 makes mistakes about what it will find appealing.

A growing literature, creating serious problems for the Epistemic Argument, explores the difference between "decision utility" and "experienced utility"—the difference between the utility that we think we will get when we make a decision and the utility we actually experience after that decision has been made.[24] The central finding is that at the time of decision, people think that they will obtain a certain amount of utility, or welfare, from certain products or activities—but they sometimes err. We might think that a very expensive car would be a joy to own, but we might get used to that car, and after a while, we might not get a lot of pleasure from it. If we relax the immediacy condition, these are plausible situations for invoking the Bridge Exception. Of course people should be allowed to buy cars even if they end up liking them less than they expect. For paternalists, the serious cases are those in which we make choices that greatly endanger our health and shorten our lives.

True, people learn, and true, pleasure is hardly the only thing that people do or should care about. We choose certain activities not because they are fun or joyful, but because they are right to choose, perhaps because they are meaningful. People want their lives to have purpose; they do not want their lives to be simply happy.[25] People sensibly, even virtuously, choose things that they will not in any simple sense "like."[26] For example, they may want to help others even when it is not a lot of fun to do that. They may want to do what they are morally obliged to do, even if they do not enjoy it. An important survey suggests that people's projected choices are *generally* based on what they believe would promote their subjective well-being—but that sometimes people are willing to make choices that would sacrifice their happiness in favor of an assortment of other goals, including (1) promoting the happiness of their family, (2) increasing their control over their lives, (3) increasing their social status, or (4) improving their sense of purpose in life.[27]

But I am speaking of cases in which people are really focusing on what they will like, and what they experience as a result of their choices is not what they hope and expect. Contrary to the Epistemic Argument, their choices do not make them happy. Those choices might even make them seriously ill (or dead). In this sense, they select the wrong means to their own ends. The unlovely technical term here is "affective forecasting errors."[28] In fact, we can easily imagine cases in which people choose certain actions explicitly on the ground that those actions are likely to be meaningful—and they turn out to be wrong. Affective forecasting errors are paralleled by many other kinds of errors, including those that involve other goods that people care about.

People might, for example, believe that a certain decision would increase the happiness of family members, but they might be entirely wrong in that belief. Consider the finding that people often choose bad Christmas presents for those they love, thus producing billions of dollars in deadweight losses every year.[29] People might believe that a certain outcome will increase their status or their sense of purpose or meaning, but they might be wrong in that belief as well. I am not aware of any empirical work on "meaningfulness forecasting errors," but I forecast that there will be one.

aternalists are correct to emphasize the importance
ing. Some imaginable forms of choice architecture,
l to welfare-promoting paternalism, might indeed in-
eople; we could easily imagine science fiction stories
n, and indeed *Brave New World* can be understood
ical example. But in terms of the initiatives under
here, the concern is more hypothetical than real. If
ent provides truthful information or offers warn-
t impeding learning. True, default rules give peo-
ath, but without default rules of various kinds,
quickly be overloaded (and less able to learn
lly concerns them). With respect to the value of
orms of paternalism might well run into strong
are energy-efficiency and fuel-economy re-
y subject to those objections, if their benefits
eir costs? With respect to infantilization and
approach is to examine concrete proposals
e objections are merely rhetorical or have

ld certainly respect heterogeneity. A cen-
ft paternalism and nudges is that they do
they allow people to go their own way.
Law.) And if hard paternalism is defen-
full accounting of costs and benefits, it
in a way that nonetheless gives maxi-

CAN TAXES MAKE YOU HAPPY?

Here is a simple but striking example of the possibility that hard paternalism can actually increase people's welfare. We would ordinarily expect people to be worse off if public officials make it more expensive for them to purchase goods that they want. If government tells you that you have to spend more to buy a computer, a book, a lamp, or a pair of shoes, your life will not be better. But there may be exceptions. More specifically, *cigarette taxes appear to make smokers happier.*[30] To the extent that this is so, it is because smoking itself makes smokers less happy. When smokers are taxed, they smoke less and may even quit—and they are better off as a result. (Historical note: In 2009, President Obama, himself a former smoker, signed a law that increased the tax on cigarettes by $0.62, from $0.39 to $1.01. Fact: Increased taxes, which are far more than a nudge, can have a big effect in reducing smoking.)

This finding is most puzzling if we are inclined to think that people's decisions always increase their welfare, or if we think that people always know best about what is good for them. If we believed that, we would hardly expect to find that people are better off if their choices are taxed and in that sense discouraged. For various reasons, including its addictive nature, smoking is, of course, a highly unusual activity. We should agree that if we want to make people better off, the best approach is hardly to increase the price of goods that they want. But smoking may not be unique. It is not unimaginable that people would be happier as a result of other taxes on goods that they choose.

Consider, for example, taxes on foods that cause obesity or other health problems.[31] At least in the abstract, there is a plausible argument that such taxes would have good effects and indeed that they would improve people's subjective well-being. True, people like tasty foods, and true, higher taxes can have a range of bad consequences. Indeed, there is evidence of such consequences from Denmark's fifteen-month experiment with a "fat tax,"[32] which appears to have failed miserably. To know whether such taxes can be justified on balance, we would have to assess the full set of costs and benefits. My only point is that there is an intelligible argument for them, even if they are not consistent with the Harm Principle. In fact, we might be able to see some taxes as analogous to commitment strategies, meant to address internalities, in which people agree to put obstacles in their own way; recall the tale of Ulysses and the Sirens.

The broadest point is that in some cases, there is real space between anticipated welfare and actual experience. The space suggests that if welfare is our guide, the antipaternalist position will run into serious problems, especially in cases that involve serious risks to life or health. Sure, it might be rescued if we invoke the Epistemic Argument and have good reason to

think that whatever the errors m
less frequent, and less damagi
public officials.[33] But that ques
vestigation, and in light of th
the Epistemic Argument is

The Antipaternal
b

We have seen that
welfarist objections
tions must be take
across-the-board
Taken individual
Principle.

Competitic
can provide
have seen th
such failur
ture, ever
than sq
tions v
tion
redi
co
i

Anti
of learn
dedicate
fantilize
in that ve
as a canon
discussion
the governr
ings, it is no
ple an easy
people would
about what re
learning, hard
objections. Bu
quirements real
greatly exceed th
learning, the bes
to test whether th
real force.

Paternalists sho
tral advantage of so
exactly that, becaus
(Return to the First
sible by reference to
should be undertaken

mum respect to freedom of choice—as, for example, through fuel-economy standards that respect that principle (for example, through the use of fleetwide averages, which give a great deal of freedom and flexibility to both companies and consumers) and through environmental regulations that allow the private sector to find its own way to achieve the relevant goals (for example, through performance standards rather than design standards). We have seen that with respect to default rules, personalized paternalism may well be best, precisely because one size does not fit all. And choice architects should acknowledge that in some contexts, active choosing is the best response to heterogeneity.

No one should neglect the fallibility of public officials, and hence the real issue is insistently comparative. The public choice problem cannot safely be ignored. But those who invoke that problem should not use it as a kind of all-purpose bludgeon against initiatives that promise to do more good than harm. Interest groups can and do have harmful effects, but that reasonable point is not sufficient to justify a refusal to respond to standard market failures of the sort that support the most conventional roles of government, such as the provision of national defense, antitrust law, environmental protection, and a system of justice committed to the rule of law (including an independent judiciary). What is true for standard market failures is true for behavioral market failures as well.

Imaginable Worlds and
Rule-Consequentialist Antipaternalism

It should now be obvious that the welfarist objections to paternalism, whatever their form, depend on empirical assumptions and perhaps even hunches. We could certainly imagine a world—call it Millville—in which the best approach, from the standpoint of welfare, is to let people decide as they see fit, and to impose a flat ban on government efforts to influence their decisions. (I am bracketing here the inevitability of choice architecture and the inevitable fact that a number of choices are inevitably made for people already.) We could also imagine a world—call it Benthamville—in which any such flat ban would be far too crude, if our goal is to increase welfare, and in which we would want to make some distinctions designed to maximize welfare by, for example, authorizing paternalism when the risks of widespread private error are especially high (and the risks of government error low), and forbidding paternalism when the risks of private error are low (and the risks of government error high).

We could even imagine a world—call it Nirvana—in which public officials could be trusted, so that the space for paternalism would be significantly increased. We could easily imagine a world—call it Taxonomy—in which the form of paternalism much mattered, so that criminal penalties would be strongly disfavored, but subsidies and taxes would be acceptable, or in which criminal penalties, subsidies, and taxes would be strongly disfavored, but in which nudges would be entirely acceptable.

Which of these worlds is our own? Reasonable people differ. Some of the strongest objections[34] offer a kind of explicit or implicit rule-consequentialism, meant to establish a general principle that preempts case-by-case inquiries. Those who make such objections acknowledge that people err and that it is possible, in principle, that public officials could promote people's welfare. But they suggest that if we want to promote welfare on balance, we should adopt a rule or at least a presumption against paternalism, whether hard or soft, and whether focused on means or ends.

The rule-consequentialist position would be supported with the following questions: Who will monitor public officials? Who will nudge them? What about the value of private learning, to ensure that (in Mill's words) people are "active and energetic," rather than "inert and torpid"?[35] I have emphasized that public officials are hardly invulnerable to the cognitive errors described here. Even if their distinctive role means that System 2 will be very much engaged, their susceptibility to private pressure raises distinctive concerns.

We have seen that the public choice problem should not be used as an all-purpose battering ram or trump card, and it is possible to identify cases in which people are better off if government is authorized to act paternalistically. But according to one view, the risks outweigh the potential gains. On that view, we should adopt a general rule against paternalism on rule-consequentialist grounds, not because the general rule always leads in good directions, but because it is far safer, and far better, than a case-by-case approach.

Choice Architecture and Inevitable Nudges

We have seen an immediate objection to the rule-consequentialist suggestion, and it cannot be repeated often enough, simply because it is so often ignored (and so please forgive the italics): *Choice architecture is inevitable.* The social environment influences choices, and it is not possible to dispense with a social environment. This point holds whether the social environment is a product of self-conscious designers or of some kind of invisible-hand mechanism. There can be (and often is) choice architecture without choice architects.[36] Default rules are omnipresent, and they matter. Do we have an opt in design or an opt-out design? Whenever there is an answer, there is an effect on outcomes.

Does this mean that paternalism is also unavoidable? Suppose that we use the definition set out above, so that paternalism is involved when public officials do not believe that people's choices will promote their welfare, and hence are taking steps to influence or alter people's choices for their own good. If so, we might think that while choice architecture cannot be avoided, it is possible to avoid paternalism. Perhaps choice architects—at least if they are working for the government—can self-consciously refuse to influence or alter people's choices (if the only concern is the effect of those choices on choosers themselves). Government officials might respect those choices, and the choice architecture that is established by the private sector, and attempt to avoid any independent effects of their own.

It is true that officials can work to minimize such effects. But some choice architecture is likely to be in place from government, and no such architecture is entirely neutral.[37] Whenever officials are setting up websites or cafeterias, or producing forms and applications of various kinds, their decisions will have some effect on what people select. Programs from the Social Security Administration, the Department of Agriculture, the Department of Energy, and the Department of Education inevitably contain choice architecture. If people have to fill out a form to receive a permit or to obtain aid (or to pay taxes), they will immediately encounter some such architecture, and it will affect their behavior.

The rule-consequentialist objection would therefore have to be more refined. It would be that government should avoid paternalism whenever it is feasible to do so. And it must be agreed that warnings and educational campaigns can be abandoned, or stopped before they start. It is also true that officials can work, in many cases, to eliminate default rules and to rely on active choosing. If we think that public officials are overwhelmingly likely to err, or to be poorly motivated, we might think that the risks of official action outweigh the benefits. This thought cannot be rejected in the abstract. In some times and places, it is undoubtedly correct.

But if we are really concerned about people's welfare, we will not rely on that abstract possibility. We will ask about costs and benefits. At least in the United States, what we know about nudges and their effects[38] makes it extremely hard to defend the rule-consequentialist objection, even in its more refined form. Would we really be better off if government did not inform people of the risks of smoking and of driving without seatbelts? Of the nutritional content of food? Of texting while driving? Should government blind itself to what it knows about behavioral market failures?

A more general point involves the relationship between System 1 and System 2. Many of the errors and biases discussed here are driven by System 1. Public officials do not exactly lack a System 1—far from it—but as I have noted, much of their job is to rely on System 2, by assessing costs and benefits and by devoting careful thought to options and consequences. We need not be naïve about this process, or think that everything is working as it should, to agree that at least in well-functioning democracies, the power of System 2, in the public domain, operates as a valuable safeguard.

To evaluate this argument, it might well be necessary to make some distinctions among political actors. Within the executive branch in the U.S. government, the long-standing requirement of attention to costs and benefits can produce a kind of System 2 safeguard against serious mistakes.[39] At the same time, elected officials, including those in Congress, may or may not be relying on careful analysis. Often they do so, of course. But in at least some cases, their own intuitive reactions, and those of their constituents, drive judgments about policy and even legislation. It is true that, in the United States, the structure of the national legislature was designed to promote careful deliberation. James Madison wrote that the Senate was "to consist in its proceedings with more coolness, with more system and with more wisdom, than the popular branch."[40] The same idea is reflected in a much-quoted exchange between Thomas Jefferson and George Washington. When Jefferson asked why the Constitutional Convention had created a Senate, Washington noted that "we pour legislation into the senatorial saucer to cool it."[41] Nonetheless (and to put the point lightly), such cooling does not always occur.

While the institutional safeguards are imperfect, my basic conclusion is that the welfarist objections to paternalism have no force when some kind of paternalism is inevitable, and in any case depend on empirical conjectures that are sometimes right and sometimes wrong. Taken singly or in combination, the objections are not decisive. When there is a behavioral market failure, and when it is causing serious harm, it is implausible—a form of evidence-free dogmatism—to say that a public response is off-limits, especially but not only if it takes the form of soft paternalism. If we are welfarists, and if we seek to make people's lives better and longer, we should take behavioral market failures seriously.

FOUR

Paternalism and Autonomy

Suppose that we believe that freedom of choice has a special and independent status. Liberty as such, and not welfare, might be our guide. We might insist that people have a right to choose and that government cannot legitimately intrude on that right even when it does in fact know best. If people want to buy twenty-four-ounce soda bottles, high-calorie food, energy-inefficient refrigerators, or cars that have poor fuel economy, they are entitled to do just that. If they want to gamble or smoke, to spend their money rather than to save it, or to exercise just once a year (perhaps the day after New Year's?), the government has no business intervening, even if those choices cause them harm.

On this view, people should not be regarded as children; they should be treated with respect.[1] They should be seen as ends, not means. Ludwig von Mises insisted that people "are the sovereign," and that the proof of this claim is "that they have *the right to be foolish*"; in his view, "freedom really means *the freedom to make mistakes.*"[2] (In both cases, the italics are his.) If government substitutes its own judgments for those of choosers, it violates these principles. The real problem, on this view, is that all forms of paternalism, including those that grow out of an understanding of behavioral market failures, threaten individual dignity and endanger liberty. Here too, however, we should make a distinction.

Autonomy: The Thin Version

The thin version of this position suggests that freedom of choice is an *ingredient* of welfare, and when we decide what government should do, we need to take account of the harmful effect, on welfare, of interfering with that freedom. On this view, people often dislike having their choices overridden, punished, or even significantly influenced; they experience a loss in welfare, and possibly a serious one. People want to choose for themselves. They believe that the right to choose has intrinsic and not merely instrumental value, in the sense that they suffer when that right is overridden. When the government tells people that they have to save money, or cannot text while driving, or have to buckle their seatbelts, it may be making them less happy, and possibly frustrated and angry.

The welfare loss that comes from eliminating choices may be large, and it has to be taken into account.

While the thin version raises serious objections to mandates and bans, it might be thought that nudges, including default rules, are not at all a problem, because people can ultimately choose however they like. If we prize the right to decide, nudges do not seem objectionable at all, because they insist on preserving that right. But if we believe that choice is a component in welfare, some kinds of nudging, including default rules, might not be entirely unobjectionable.[3] With a default rule, people are automatically placed in a certain situation unless they opt out. If people like to choose, perhaps it would be better to have a regime of active choosing, avoiding default rules altogether and simply asking people what they want. One advantage of this approach is that people's choices may well promote their welfare better than those of public officials (the Epistemic Argument). Another advantage is that choosing promotes learning. Yet another advantage—and the one that I am emphasizing here—is that many people like choosing as such. True, default rules allow people to make a choice if they really want to do that. But active choosing directly engages people, as default rules do not, and people might like it better for that very reason.

In some contexts, the thin version is certainly correct. When people enjoy freedom of choice and suffer when it is overridden, that loss must be counted in the overall assessment. If people want to select their own retirement plans, or hate the idea of being forced to buckle their seatbelts or to wear motorcycle helmets, public officials should consider those desires. Empirical research suggests that people do indeed believe that decision rights have intrinsic value,[4] apart from their instrumental value, and when this is so, the welfare effects of compromising those rights must be taken into account. Evidence of this kind provides a good reason for maintaining freedom of choice and for favoring nudges over mandates and bans.

It is important, however, to see that on the thin version, freedom of choice is relevant but not necessarily decisive. The thin version is welfarist; it simply adds (the important point) that freedom of choice may be a significant ingredient in the welfare calculus. Under the thin version, the welfare gain of the paternalist action may outweigh the welfare loss. (True, the measurement issues are formidable here.) Perhaps people would feel frustrated, but perhaps the frustration would be mild, and perhaps their lives would be much longer and much better.

It is also important to see that in some contexts, people do not enjoy freedom of choice and would much prefer not to have to spend time on the question at all.[5] Especially in complex and unfamiliar domains, active choosing can be a burden, not a benefit. Whether people feel frustrated by a denial of choice, or instead relieved and grateful, depends on the context. There are also issues about the extent to which active choosing increases or decreases satisfaction with ultimate choices. I will return to these points.

Autonomy: The Thick Version

The thick version of the autonomy position stresses not that freedom of choice is part of welfare but that it is an end in itself and thus decisive—or at least a very weighty matter, to be overridden only for the most compelling reasons.[6] To treat people with respect, and as ends rather than mere means, government cannot override that form of freedom even if doing so would, in fact, make people happier or better off in a relevant sense. On the thick version, imposing costs on those who exercise freedom of choice, or steering people in government's preferred directions, is at least presumptively unacceptable as such. Freedom of choice has intrinsic value not only in the sense that most of us independently value the right to choose (the thin version), but also and more fundamentally because human beings have dignity, and are entitled to do as they wish.

Many of the most intensely felt objections to paternalism, strong or weak, are based on an intuition or judgment of this kind. Those objections often take the form of a question: By what right can government attempt to alter the choices of free adults? On this view, people have a right to choose as they see fit, even if their choices end up doing them no good and considerable harm. This point might hold even if we do not emphasize the value of learning and of developing one's tastes and preferences.

Does this objection come from System 1? Welfarists think so, or more precisely, they believe that System 2 is asking in its capacity as System 1's lawyer or public relations manager. They insist that forceful as it is, the thick version of the autonomy objection is a rhetorical flourish and therefore unhelpful. I will return to this issue as well.

Thin, Again

Begin with the thin version. Suppose that freedom of choice is part of what people care about. Suppose too that if people are denied freedom of choice, they will suffer a loss in welfare, in part because they feel frustrated and mistreated. To the extent that this is so, there will be a legitimate and potentially forceful objection, on grounds of welfare, to hard paternalism, and we will be inclined to reject paternalism altogether (or perhaps to favor choice-preserving nudges).

BALANCING

As I have noted, it is important to see that the point may not be decisive. Perhaps people are only mildly distressed to lose freedom of choice; perhaps they are not distressed at all and consider such freedom a burden, certainly (but not only) in new or unfamiliar contexts. Their judgment to this effect need not be because they are mere sheep and do not value freedom as such. It may be because they have far better things to do and very reasonably do not want to be bothered. As I have emphasized, nudges are entirely compatible with the thin version of the autonomy argument. In some contexts, people welcome a default rule, which makes life simpler and easier, and which might protect them against their own mistakes. Experimental evidence strongly suggests that people do in fact welcome many nudges, including those that do not call for conscious deliberation, at least when they are aware that they face some kind of self-control problem or are otherwise prone to error.[7] In the words of one of the authors of the relevant study, "Apparently, autonomy is not quite as exalted a value as libertarians might believe. . . . When people recognized that their objectives in life aligned with the nudge *and knew that they were struggling with achieving that objective*, they generally endorsed the nudge. . . . When people are self-aware enough to recognize that they need help, when they understand the inherent weakness of their own will, autonomy takes a back seat."[8]

In unfamiliar or complex situations, default rules are unlikely to run afoul of the thin version of the autonomy argument (at least if they are well designed). If, for example, the question is the precise content of a retirement plan, some people might be delighted if the employer selects a plan that meets their needs (subject of course to the right to opt out), and the issue does not seem much different if the employer is the federal or state government. Or perhaps the welfare gain from influencing or even overriding choice is very large, because people would choose in a way that would cause them serious harm. Consider bans on suicide. To be sure, some people strongly oppose such bans, but there is a strong argument that in numerous cases, people who are impulsive, or who are facing acute short-term distress, are tempted to engage in an action that reflects the power of System 1, and that it is best to use the force of law to strengthen the hand of System 2.

The thin version of the autonomy argument raises an important and highly relevant question, one that may argue against hard paternalism and in favor of active choosing. But it is an empirical issue whether that question, properly answered, raises a serious problem for a proposed act of paternalism.

CHOICE ARCHITECTURE AND FREEDOM

Actually, there is a deeper problem, to which I briefly referred in the context of welfare: All of us could, in principle, make far more decisions than we do in fact. Every hour of every day, choices are implicitly made for us, by both private and public institutions, and we are both better off and more autonomous as a result. If we had to make all decisions that are relevant to us, without the assistance of helpful choice architecture, we would be far less free. In a literal sense, choice architecture enables us to be free.

Most of us do not have to make choices about what a refrigerator or an alarm clock should look like, or how best to clean tap water, or how to build or fly an airplane, or what safety equipment should be on trains, or what medicine to take if we have strep throat, or whether chemotherapy should exist, or where highways and street signs are located. Time is limited, and some issues are complex, boring, or both. If we did not benefit from an explicit or implicit delegation of choice-making authority to others, we would be far worse off, and in an important sense less autonomous, because we would have far less time to chart our own course. Autonomy itself depends on a social background, many of whose basic ingredients we need to be able to take for granted. Without that background, and if active choosing were required for everything, our autonomy would quickly evaporate.

In a statement that deserves to be widely known, Esther Duflo, one of the world's leading experts on poverty, says the following:

[W]e tend to be patronizing about the poor in a very specific sense, which is that we tend to think, "Why don't they take more responsibility for their lives?" And what we are forgetting is that the richer you are the less responsibility you need to take for your own life because everything is taken care for you. And the poorer you are the more you have to be responsible for everything about your life.... [S]top berating people for not being responsible and start to think of ways instead of providing the poor with the luxury that we all have, which is that a lot of decisions are taken for us. If we do nothing, we are on the right track. For most of the poor, if they do nothing, they are on the wrong track.[9]

Duflo's central claim is that people who are well off do not have to be responsible for a wide range of things, because others are making the relevant decisions, and to their benefit. Recall David Foster Wallace's "what's water?" joke. Rich people swim in clean water, and they don't have to think about it; indeed, they might not even notice it. Those who are well off need not take burdensome steps to ensure that that their water, food, and streets are safe. We need not focus in particular on the disparity between rich and poor to see that as a matter of fact, decisions are taken for all of us by both private and public institutions.

Of course it is exceedingly important that we can revisit (many of) those decisions if we do not like them. But if we had to make all relevant choices in the first instance, we would be worse off—and far less free—as a result. Because people feel frustrated if their autonomy is compromised, choice-preserving approaches are usually best. But it is also important to recognize that many aspects of the prevailing choice architecture are fixed, and we cannot easily opt out of them.

Thick, Again

The thick version of the autonomy argument does not turn on empirical questions, and it is, in a sense, a show-stopper. If people have to be treated as ends rather than as mere means, and if this principle requires government not to influence private choices on paternalistic grounds, there is not a lot of room for further discussion. We might be forced to acknowledge that if we accept a certain view of autonomy, actions that fall in the category of hard paternalism are presumptively out of bounds. In such cases, those who believe in autonomy will insist that government needs an exceptionally strong reason to interfere with private choices. But what about soft paternalism and nudges? Is there anything insulting or demeaning about automatic enrollment in savings and health care plans, accompanied by unconstrained opt-out rights? Which nudges, and which forms of libertarian paternalism, interfere with autonomy, rightly understood? Surely disclosure policies are not an objectionable interference with autonomy; a GPS does not compromise liberty. Does government really treat people as mere means when it uses default rules to promote better choices?

Perhaps we can agree that in some cases, the interest in autonomy does justify a preference for active choosing rather than a default rule. But in all contexts? What if the area is highly technical, and people would consider active choosing a burden rather than a benefit, and a default rule would reduce the number and magnitude of errors?

Let me venture a stronger, more direct, and perhaps reckless response to those who invoke autonomy.[10] On one view, what really does and should matter is welfare, for which claims about autonomy are best understood as a heuristic (at least in the areas under discussion here). More precisely, autonomy is what matters to System 1, but on reflection, the real concern, vindicated by System 2, is welfare. People speak in terms of autonomy, but what they are doing is making a rapid, intuitive judgment about welfare. Often they are moved by the Epistemic Argument, but they invoke autonomy instead, even though it is not their real concern. On this view, objections from autonomy are far from pointless, and for one reason: When we vindicate autonomy, we generally promote welfare. But on this view, it is much better, and much less crude, to focus directly on welfare. And on this view, autonomy disintegrates as an independent argument (except insofar as we are speaking of the thin version). The real question involves welfare.

This possibility suggests that we need a kind of behavioral science for judgments of morality, and not merely judgments of fact.[11] Moral heuristics are pervasive, and they can go wrong, no less than heuristics of other kinds. Consider an analogy: The availability heuristic helps people to come up with estimates of probability, and it generally works well. When we learn of an incident in which certain actions produced serious harm, we update our probability judgments. The updating is perfectly sensible. Use of the availability heuristic can be seen as a kind of rough-and-ready statistical analysis—and perhaps it is even better than that. The problem is that use of the availability heuristic can also go badly wrong, leading to wildly exaggerated fears (or to unhealthy complacency). The same problems arise for many moral heuristics, which generally work well but can lead us in bad directions.

Consider this heuristic: Do not lie. The prohibition on lying is a heuristic, and for most of us, System 1 has thoroughly internalized it, so that whatever the circumstances, a lie produces distress and perhaps even a physical reaction (such as a rapid heartbeat and sweaty hands). To the extent that lie detectors tend to work, that is why. But System 2 knows that lying is sometimes acceptable and even obligatory, as when it is necessary to save a life. ("No one is with me," says the parent of the kidnapping victim to the kidnapper, as she brings a police officer to the scene.) What I am suggesting is that in many contexts, the objection from autonomy may be a heuristic and that what we really should care about is welfare.

Defending their preferred approach, some utilitarians have

spoken in analogous terms, arguing that commonsense morality is composed of a series of heuristics for what matters, which is utility. Emphasizing that utilitarianism is broadly compatible with commonsense morality, Henry Sidgwick urges:

> It may be shown, I think, that the Utilitarian estimate of consequences not only supports broadly the current moral rules, but also sustains their generally received limitations and qualifications: that, again, it explains anomalies in the Morality of Common Sense, which from any other point of view must seem unsatisfactory to the reflective intellect; and moreover, where the current formula is not sufficiently precise for the guidance of conduct, while at the same time difficulties and perplexities arise in the attempt to give it additional precision, the Utilitarian method solves these difficulties and perplexities in general accordance with the vague instincts of Common Sense, and is naturally appealed to for such solution in ordinary moral discussions.[12]

In the same vein, it might be urged that when we respect autonomy, we generally promote welfare, and when we assess paternalism, welfare is what matters. While I believe that this suggestion is generally correct, I have acknowledged that it may be reckless, and there are many possible responses to it. On a competing view, System 1 speaks in terms of welfare, and

System 2 is able to make the case for autonomy.[13] Certainly many pages have been devoted to the elaboration of what autonomy requires, with System 2 working overtime on that project.[14] Those who invoke autonomy do not by any means rest content with their intuitions; they justify their views. Perhaps human beings have immediate intuitions about both welfare and autonomy, and the real question is how best to evaluate those intuitions.[15] As we learn more about the operation of the brain, it may be possible to make progress on these issues, and there is some suggestive (if preliminary) evidence that System 1 is distinctly associated with an emphasis on the importance of autonomy.[16]

To say the least, those who emphasize autonomy, and who accept the thick version, are not at all likely to be convinced by what I am calling my reckless suggestion. Let us take the objection on its own terms. It bears repeating that in ordinary life, choice architecture ensures that we do not have to make countless imaginable decisions. Of course we are allowed to participate in markets and to vote, and in these ways, we are able to influence choice architecture of multiple kinds. In many contexts, we can opt out. But our autonomy is promoted, not undermined, by the existence of helpful choice architecture, ensuring that if we do not make particular decisions, we will be just fine. If we had to make far more decisions, our autonomy would be badly compromised, because we would be unable to focus on what concerns us. This is not a point about heuristics. It is a point about the limitations of time, interest, and attention.[17]

If we emphasize autonomy, we are not likely to reject nudges as such. Certainly we will not question reasonable efforts to ensure that people are adequately informed. If they are accurate, warnings should be perfectly legitimate. Active choosing is sometimes best, but default rules are not off-limits, certainly if such rules reflect the likely choices of informed people. So long as freedom of choice is maintained, and government does not impose significant costs on those who seek to go their own way, autonomy is not undermined.

Suppose that we stipulate that governments should not treat people merely as means. Nudges, including information disclosure, do not run afoul of that prescription. On the contrary, disclosure itself promotes autonomy, by allowing individuals to make informed decisions about their own ends.

The chief response to those who invoke autonomy, then, is that reasonable responses to behavioral market failures ought not to raise serious concerns, certainly not if they respect the First Law of Behaviorally Informed Regulation and take the form of nudges. And in some cases, even harder forms of paternalism may not run afoul of autonomy concerns, at least if they respect people's ends. Consider fuel-economy standards, at least if they are based on fleetwide averages, and allow a diverse array of vehicles to continue to be available to consumers.

mote energy security by reducing dependence on foreign oil, the justification also involves externalities. But as noted, the strong majority of the benefits from such rules do not involve air pollution or energy security. They involve consumer savings, in the form of reduced costs from use.

Should those savings be counted in the analysis of what to do? On one view, they should not be. There is a market for fuel economy and for energy efficiency. Consumers can trade off the relevant values as they see fit. They can certainly purchase cars with excellent fuel economy. If they are willing to spend more on the initial purchase in order to save on gas costs over time, the market allows them ample opportunity. And if they want more fuel economy than the market now provides, they can push the market in that direction. Markets, no less than government, can be technology-forcing.

On the other hand, consumer savings from fuel-efficient cars and from energy-efficient appliances unquestionably count as benefits. They represent savings to consumers, brought about by regulation. The hard question is not whether they count as benefits, but identification of the relevant market failure. We have seen that a behavioral account, offered by the Department of Transportation and the Environmental Protection Agency, emphasizes both myopia and salience. The argument here is grounded in the idea of an Energy Paradox, in which consumers do not purchase energy-efficient goods even though it is in their economic interest to do so.[19] Insofar as myopia and salience are the foundations of policy, a form of behaviorally informed paternalism is involved, and it is not soft.

These points suggest the circumstances in which a mandate, rather than a nudge, might be the right response to a behavioral market failure. If the benefits of the mandate plainly outweigh the costs, it would seem justified, at least if that assessment can be trusted, and if there is no real problem from the standpoint of autonomy. Of course the costs include any welfare loss experienced by those who are not allowed to choose. If a mandate would have significantly higher benefits than a nudge, there may well be a convincing argument for it, at least if it does not also have significantly higher costs. Choice architects should consult the antipaternalist's quintet (see chapter 3) to decide whether and when mandates are justified.

I have argued that the best responses to behavioral market failures usually involve nudges, which preserve freedom of choice. But I have also suggested that the master concept is social welfare, and that when the benefits justify the costs, harder forms of paternalism are not off-limits. The areas of fuel economy and energy efficiency are plausible examples. Others include food safety standards, workplace safety regulations, and prescription-only medicines. If the argument here is correct, these measures should not be ruled out of bounds simply because they are paternalistic. The question depends on their consequences.

FIVE

Soft Paternalism and Its Discontents

The argument thus far has proceeded on the assumption that hard paternalism raises special problems and that soft paternalism is usually better along important dimensions. If paternalistic approaches impose small costs, or no material costs, on those who seek to go their own way, then such approaches are far less vulnerable to the objections I have discussed here. The central reason is that they preserve freedom of choice. Some of those approaches might be compatible with the Harm Principle (consider warnings), and even if they are not (consider certain default rules), the right to opt out creates an important safety valve, one that should alleviate some of the concerns of those who invoke welfare, autonomy, or both.

At the same time, soft paternalism and nudging do run into

three potentially special concerns, and they should be addressed independently. The first involves transparency. The second involves the risk of manipulation. The third (applicable to both soft and hard paternalism) involves the legitimate claims of System 1. There are also questions about the relationship between illicit motivations and soft paternalism.

Of Transparency, Visibility, and Political Safeguards

Mandates and commands are highly visible, and government is likely to be held accountable for them. If public officials tax cigarettes or soft drinks, impose new energy-efficiency requirements on refrigerators, forbid people from riding motorcycles without helmets, or require them to buckle their seatbelts, nothing is mysterious, hidden, or secret. The prohibitions may or may not be acceptable, but they lack the distinctive vice of insidiousness. No one is confused or fooled. Political safeguards are triggered. The government must defend itself publicly. And if the public defense is perceived as weak, the proposed action may well crumble. In a democracy, officials are subject to public scrutiny whenever they impose mandates and bans.

It is important to be careful with this argument. One person's political safeguard will be another person's interest-group power. If a mandate is vulnerable as a matter of political reality, it may not be because "the people" are unhappy. It may be because a self-interested private group is at risk and seeking to block a desirable measure. If a potentially lifesaving policy runs into trouble because its visibility triggers opprobrium and threats of political reprisal, we do not know that it is necessarily bad, and we should not take the trouble as proof of its badness. Even in a well-functioning democracy, it is important not to romanticize the world of political checks; recall the public choice problem. Nonetheless, it is true that government must be accountable to the public, and visibility is, in general, an important and desirable safeguard.

This point is closely related to one made by the great Supreme Court Justice Robert Jackson.[1] Insisting on the importance of requiring the laws to be applied generally, he famously wrote:

> I regard it as a salutary doctrine that cities, states and the Federal Government must exercise their powers so as not to discriminate between their inhabitants except upon some reasonable differentiation fairly related to the object of regulation. This equality is not merely abstract justice. The framers of the Constitution knew, and we should not forget today, that there is no more effective practical guaranty against arbitrary and unreasonable government than to require that the principles of law which officials would impose upon a minority must be

imposed generally. Conversely, nothing opens the door to arbitrary action so effectively as to allow those officials to pick and choose only a few to whom they will apply legislation and thus to escape the political retribution that might be visited upon them if larger numbers were affected. Courts can take no better measure to assure that laws will be just than to require that laws be equal in operation.[2]

Justice Jackson's argument, in short, is that generality is a corrective against abuse, because laws that apply generally trigger political safeguards. Friedrich Hayek wrote in similar terms, arguing that selective impositions—on, for example, religious minorities—are especially troublesome because officials can impose them without much fearing political retribution.[3] By contrast, Hayek contended that general impositions trigger democratic safeguards and hence are less likely to be put in place unless they are well justified. Indeed, Hayek's conception of the rule of law relies heavily on this point. In his view, the rule of law itself requires generality and forbids selectivity.

We should reiterate that the existence of interest groups significantly weakens the force of such arguments. Nonetheless, political safeguards are exceedingly important, and a similar point can be made about the transparency of mandates and bans, which also trigger such safeguards. On this count, some people think that soft paternalism does not fare so well.[4] Precisely because of its subtlety and softness, such paternalism—and some nudges in particular—may be invisible. They may be manipulative.[5] They may even be self-insulating insofar as they alter the very behavior, and perhaps the public beliefs and understandings, that would otherwise be brought to bear against them. And indeed, prominent critics of soft paternalism have suggested that the lack of transparency is a serious problem. In the words of the economist Edward Glaeser:

> Hard paternalism generally involves measurable instruments. The public can observe the size of sin taxes and voters can tell that certain activities have been outlawed. Rules can be set in advance about how far governments can go in pursuing their policies of hard paternalism. Effective soft paternalism must be situation-specific and creative in the language of its message. This fact makes soft paternalism intrinsically difficult to control and means that it is, at least on these grounds, more subject to abuse than hard paternalism.[6]

The underlying concern must be taken seriously, and the best response is simple. For Glaeser's reasons, nothing should be hidden, and everything should be transparent.[7] Soft paternalism, nudges, and any other behaviorally informed approaches, no less than hard paternalism, should be visible, scrutinized, and monitored. To the extent feasible, practices that embody soft paternalism should be subject to public scrutiny in advance, often through notice-and-comment rule-making. Consider some initiatives: automatic enrollment in savings and health care plans; the substitution of the Food Plate for the Food Pyramid; the revised fuel-economy label and other disclosure policies that reflect how people actually process information; Mayor Bloomberg's Big Gulp effort; graphic health warnings; cafeterias that make healthful food more visible and accessible; fuel-economy standards. All of these initiatives are visible, public, and entirely observable. All were, and remain, subject to public scrutiny. None is "intrinsically difficult to control." In this light, what is the problem?

Perhaps we can answer by offering a behavioral twist on Glaeser's argument. Perhaps the problem is not so much a lack of transparency as a lack of salience. Perhaps the objection is not that the government keeps behaviorally informed initiatives secret, but that those initiatives do not attract the kinds of attention that are typically triggered by mandates and bans.

So understood, the objection is certainly plausible insofar as it is applies to actions of government that, while hardly hidden, lack the kinds of salience that produce careful public scrutiny. Salience matters for laws and regulation as for everything else. The problem is that nudges and soft paternalism are often highly salient, and the line between what is salient and what is not is hardly the same as the line between hard paternalism and soft paternalism. Consider, for example, graphic warnings for cigarettes, which received considerable public scrutiny and attention, and the current fuel-economy labels, which were also highly salient to the public. A lack of salience does create a problem for those who emphasize political safeguards, but soft paternalism may be exceptionally salient. There is nothing intrinsic to nudging that reduces salience.

But there is another way of understanding the basic concern. Some nudges promote conscious deliberation.[8] A requirement of calorie labeling has that feature; the same is true of disclosure of the annual fuel costs of motor vehicles. In such cases, the relevant nudge attempts to inform people's choices, perhaps by counteracting System 1, and certainly by engaging System 2. We could imagine a wide range of nudges whose explicit purpose is to promote self-conscious deliberation about consequences (and in that sense to promote autonomy and to avoid any semblance of manipulation). Active choosing is the paradigm example here.

By contrast, some nudges do not promote deliberation at all, and instead enlist behavioral findings in a way that can be seen to operate "behind the back" of the chooser. A default rule can be understood in these terms; it enlists inertia and need not spur conscious deliberation. We have seen that a cafeteria or grocery store might make some items more visible (fruits and vegetables?) and others less so (chocolate cake?), and perhaps hide still others (cigarettes?). We have also seen that the order of items matters, and so people might be nudged by placing certain options at the end of a long list (or in a small font). In a similar vein, people tend to think that green items are healthier, and indeed, health-conscious consumers are more likely to buy candy in green wrappers (even if it has no health benefits); choice architects might use color to spur (what they consider to be) preferable choices. In all of these cases, the goal is not to encourage conscious deliberation or to activate System 2. It is to produce certain outcomes by influencing or appealing to System 1.

Nudges that do not spur deliberation need not be secret or covert, but they might be taken to raise special concerns. And indeed, evidence suggests that people are generally more comfortable with deliberation-promoting nudges than with those that seem to work more subconsciously.[9] People appear to think that after deliberation occurs, their decisions are more authentically theirs. At the same time, there is only a modest difference between people's support for deliberation-promoting nudges and their support for other kinds, and many people do support the latter, at least when they believe that the consequence will be to overcome some kind of self-control problem or otherwise to promote their own ends. On these questions, more empirical research would be highly desirable.

Apart from public reactions, should nudges be seen as objectionable, as a matter of principle, if they do not promote deliberation and work only or largely because of the operations of System 1? It is hard to see why. Any cafeteria or grocery store has to have a design; any list of items has to have an order; any food wrapper has to have a color. We cannot avoid influences on System 1. In many contexts, it is indeed best to promote conscious deliberation, but so long as the initiatives are made public and defended on their merits, nudges should not be ruled off-limits merely because they work as a result of the operations of System 1.

OF EASY REVERSIBILITY

In imposing very low costs, or in failing to impose material costs, on choices, soft paternalism differs from mandates and bans. Because of the absence of such costs, soft paternalism appears to be *easily reversible.*

For example, graphic warnings do not override individual choice, and while they are not neutral and are meant to steer, people can ignore them if they want. We can easily imagine, and even find, graphic warnings that are meant to discourage texting while driving, smoking, abortion, premarital sex, and gambling. However powerful, such warnings can be ignored. Even if grocery stores put fruits and vegetables at the front and cigarettes and high-calorie foods at the back, people can always go to the back. A default rule in favor of automatic enrollment—in a savings or health insurance plan or a privacy policy—will greatly affect outcomes, and it may be decisive for many of us. But we can always opt out.

Does this mean that so long as soft paternalism or a nudge is involved, no one should worry about paternalism, or indeed about any abuse of authority or power? The answer is no. It is easy to identify an important problem with the idea of easy reversibility: the very biases and decisional inadequacies that I have traced here suggest that even when reversibility is easy in theory, it may prove difficult in practice. In part because of the power of System 1, soft paternalism may turn out to be decisive.

True, we can search for chocolate candy and cigarettes at the back of the store, and true, we might opt out of a website policy that authorizes a lot of tracking (perhaps with a simple click)—but because of the power of inertia, many of us are unlikely to do so. Graphic warnings, which appeal directly to System 1, may be exceedingly effective precisely because they target identifiable features of human cognition. The idea of easy reversibility might, in these circumstances, seem a bit of rhetoric, even a fraud—comforting, to be sure, but perhaps not a realistic response to those who are concerned about potential errors or bad faith on the part of soft paternalists and nudgers.

This objection has force. It would be wrong to suggest that because of easy reversibility, all risks are eliminated. Magazine subscribers who no longer enjoy the magazines to which they subscribe, but whose subscriptions are automatically renewed, often fail to take the trouble to discontinue them. (I speak from experience.) If people are defaulted into exploitative pension plans (with high fees and little diversification), or expensive health insurance programs that poorly fit their situations, it is not enough to say that they can go their own way if they choose to do so. If a website allows you to opt out of a privacy policy that allows it to track all of your movements on the Internet, you might well ignore the issue or say, "Yeah, whatever," and not alter the default.

In view of the fact that many people do not opt out even when it is simple to do so, a self-interested or malevolent government could easily use default rules to move people in its preferred directions. If we accept very strong assumptions about the likelihood of government mistake and about the virtues of private choice (uninfluenced by government), we might regard opt-out as an illusory safeguard and for that reason reject some forms of soft paternalism.

It remains true, however, that insofar as it maintains freedom of choice, soft paternalism is less intrusive and less dangerous than mandates and bans. This is so even if people will exercise that freedom less often than they would if inertia and procrastination were not powerful forces. While default rules matter, it is important to emphasize the empirical finding that in the face of bad or harmful defaults, a number of people will in fact opt out. We know that if people are defaulted into a retirement plan that puts a lot of their money into savings while giving them too little right now, they will indeed reject the default.[10] If people are defaulted into a health insurance plan that works out very badly for them, many of them are going to switch. When people really dislike a default rule, they might well reject it. For that reason, liberty of choice is a real safeguard.

The freedom to opt out is no panacea. But it is exceedingly important.

WHAT MAKES LIFE WORTH LIVING? THE LEGITIMATE CLAIMS OF SYSTEM I

Here is a way to understand one of the central claims made here. Often because of System 1, people err. We need to strengthen the hand of System 2 by promoting self-control, reducing unrealistic optimism, unshrouding attributes, counteracting biases, and eliminating an undue focus on the short term. Some forms of paternalism move people in the directions that they would go if they were fully rational. Paternalism, whether hard or soft, creates "as if" rationality. Indeed, that is a central point of good choice architecture.

It would be possible to object that if this approach is understood in a certain way, it ignores the legitimate claims of System 1.[11] More bluntly, it disregards what is most important in human life. People like to fall in love, even when it is pretty risky to do that. Many of our favorite foods are fattening. To be sure, most people care about their health, but unless they are fanatical, their health is not the only thing they care about. Many people like to drink and to smoke. Many of us care more about current consumption than consumption twenty years from now. When people enjoy their lives, it is because of System 1. The future matters, but the present matters too, and people reasonably and legitimately strike their own balance. As Mill wrote, "desires and impulses are as much a part of a perfect human being, as beliefs and restraints; and strong impulses are only perilous when not properly balanced."[12]

Isn't it System 1 that makes life worth living? Why should public officials, or anyone else, make people focus on something other than what they want to focus on, and promote choice architecture that devalues, denigrates, and undermines some of their most fundamental motivations and concerns? Indeed, might not System 2 be paralyzed if it lacks a sense of those concerns? How will it know what to do?

Consider a patient of Antonio Damasio, who suffered from brain damage that prevented him from experiencing emotions.[13] Because the patient lacked "gut reactions," he could perform some tasks well; for example, he was able to drive safely on icy roads, avoiding the natural reaction to hit the brakes during a skid. On the other hand, his ability to focus on consequences was accompanied by extreme difficulty in making decisions:

I was discussing with the same patient when his next visit to the laboratory should take place. I suggested two alternative dates, both in the coming month and just a few days apart from each other. The patient pulled out his appointment book and began consulting the calendar. . . . For the better part of a half-hour, the patient enumerated reasons for and against each of the two dates: previous engagements, proximity to other engagements, possible meteorological conditions, virtually anything that one could reasonably think about concerning a single date. Just as calmly as he had driven over the ice, and recounted that episode, he was now walking us through a tiresome cost-benefit analysis, an endless outlining and fruitless comparison of options and possible consequences. . . .

[We] finally did tell him, quietly, that he should come on the second of the alternative dates. His response was equally calm and prompt. He simply said: "That's fine."[14]

Without emotions, and without System 1, we might be endlessly listing consequences while lacking a motivation for choosing among them.

The underlying questions are legitimate, and they suggest the problems with some imaginable nudges, not to mention hard paternalism. At the same time, they reflect a fundamental misunderstanding of the argument made here, and the approaches that it supports. To see why, we need to make a distinction between two different understandings of the kinds of biases and errors that choice architects might counteract.

I have mentioned Mr. Spock of the old *Star Trek* show, and the first view might be associated with him. (Aficionados might consider this the Vulcan view, after Mr. Spock's logic-dominated planet.) On that view, an understanding of bounded rationality and of cognitive biases suggests that System 2 needs to be put firmly in charge. To the extent that it is not, choice architecture should be established to move people to a situation of "as if" System 2 primacy. This view raises many puzzles, because some of the greatest pleasures of life appeal directly to System 1. No sensible private or public institution would be indifferent to the fact that for sufficient reasons, people take risks because that is what they like to do. They fall in love; they overeat; they stay up all night; they get drunk; they act on impulse; they run with apparently unpromising ideas; they experiment in a million and one different ways.

On a less ambitious view, bounded rationality and cognitive biases lead people to make what they themselves see as serious errors, or would see as serious errors after reflection, and choice architecture should be established to help make those errors less likely or less damaging. If inertia leads people not to take action that (they do or would agree, if properly informed) is in their interest, then inertia might be enlisted to promote outcomes that (they do or would agree, if properly informed) are in their interest. If a problem of self-control is leading people to endanger their health, and if they do or would (if properly informed) want private and public institutions to help to solve that problem (and not to exploit it), then there is no cause for complaint if they do so.

We need not denigrate the legitimate claims of System 1 in order to accept these points. The real problem lies not in any question of high principle, but in identifying what people do or would want, and in deciding whether choice architects can be trusted. Perhaps choice architects do not know what people would want, if properly informed, and perhaps their own motivations are not pure. Perhaps the very idea of what people would want, if properly informed, raises difficult conceptual puzzles, at least in some cases, and creates unacceptable risks of overreaching by choice architects.

With respect to issues of this kind, there are limits to how much progress can be made in the abstract. We need to ask concrete questions about concrete problems. We could imagine forms of paternalism that would be objectionable because they would neglect what people really care about. Consider the Suffer Now, Celebrate When You're Almost Dead Pension Plan, automatically putting 51 percent of employee salaries into savings; or the Miserable Wellness Program, asking employees to commit to a grueling and unpleasant daily exercise regime; or the Joyless Cafeteria, keeping the tastiest foods relatively hidden. We could also imagine paternalistic approaches that are helpful rather than harmful. The challenge is to avoid the latter and promote the former.

The Problem of Impermissible Motivations

I have emphasized that soft paternalism does not impose material costs on choices. Even so, it is correct to object that this point is not conclusive, and that some forms of soft paternalism would go beyond the appropriate line. The most objectionable cases reflect not unacceptable paternalism but an altogether different problem: *impermissible motivations.* Indeed, many of the strongest intuitive objections to paternalism, even in its soft form, involve examples, real or imagined, in which government is acting on the basis of impermissible factors (potentially in violation of the Constitution itself). The objections are right, but the real problem has nothing to do with paternalism.[15]

We would not, for example, want to authorize government to default people into voting for incumbents by saying that unless they explicitly indicate otherwise, or actually show up at the ballot booth, they are presumed to vote for incumbents. Or suppose that government declared that for purposes of the census, citizens will be presumed to be Christian or Caucasian, unless they explicitly state otherwise. Some imaginable information campaigns would be unacceptable for the same reason. Suppose that government decided to inform people about all the misdeeds committed by members of a particular religious faith (say, Catholics or Jews). Or suppose that government decided to use vivid images to persuade people to choose products manufactured by its favorite interest groups.

In all of these cases, the problem does not lie with paternalism. The problem is the illegitimate or illicit ends that official paternalism, even if soft, is meant to produce. In a free and democratic society, government is not supposed to use the basic rules of voting to entrench itself, to favor certain racial and religious groups, to stigmatize members of a particular faith, or to tell people to buy the products that favored interest groups manufacture. When the government's ends are illicit, paternalism, designed to promote those ends, is illicit too.

We can imagine cases in which the illicit nature of the government's ends is clear; the examples given above are meant to be such cases. But we can also imagine cases about which people might disagree. Suppose, for example, that government were to engage in soft paternalism—say, through an aggressive educational campaign—designed to discourage people from having sex outside of marriage. Some people might think that efforts of this kind would be illicit, because they would violate a commitment to a certain kind of neutrality. Perhaps those people are right; perhaps not. The central question is whether the government's ends are illicit. It is not about paternalism.

The examples of illicit ends are important because they identify some limits on even minimally intrusive forms of paternalism. But with respect to the issues under discussion here, they are uninformative, because they do not establish the central claim, which is that certain forms of paternalism are objectionable as such. If some people are strongly committed to that claim, it is not clear what might be said to dislodge that commitment. Is it really an insult to autonomy and dignity to provide graphic images of the harms associated with cigarette smoking? To take steps to promote a norm in favor of healthful eating or against texting while driving? For those who think so, the risk is that high-sounding abstractions are being enlisted to contest initiatives that insult no one's dignity and that reflect public commitments to both compassion and respect.

Epilogue: The Lives We Save May Be Our Own

My goal here has been to explore the relationship between behavioral economics and paternalism, and in the process to cast doubt on Mill's Harm Principle. I have suggested that the Epistemic Argument is sometimes wrong and that other defenses of the Harm Principle offer cautionary notes, not a trump card. If properly confined, paternalistic measures, designed to promote people's welfare (as they understand it), embody appealing moral principles.

More particularly, I have urged that accumulating evidence suggests, more concretely than ever before, that in identifiable cases, people's mistaken choices can produce serious harm, even when there is no risk to others. The result is a series of behavioral market failures that provide a plausible basis for some kind of official remedy. Behaviorally informed responses need not, and generally should not, attempt to revisit people's ends. They are focused on correcting mistakes that people make in choosing the means to satisfy their own ends.

I have also emphasized the First (and only) Law of Behaviorally Informed Regulation, which is that the appropriate responses to behavioral market failures generally consist of nudges, typically in the form of disclosure, warnings, and default rules. But social welfare is the master concept, and in some cases, a stronger response may be justified after careful consideration of benefits and costs.

Many people object to paternalism on grounds of autonomy. I have raised the possibility that objections from autonomy are a heuristic for what really matters, which is welfare. Even if this argument is unconvincing—and I have only gestured toward it here—the most sensible responses to behavioral market failures do not run afoul of autonomy, properly conceived, certainly not if they take the form of nudges.

The most forceful objections are welfarist in character. For a variety of reasons, the cure may be worse than the disease. Indeed, the disease itself may produce long-term benefits, not least in the form of learning. At the same time, we have seen that choice architecture is inevitable, whether or not it is intentional or a product of any kind of conscious design. We have also seen that the strongest objections to hard paternalism are weaker when applied to soft paternalism.

Many of the most plausible arguments against paternalism

depend on empirical claims that may not be true. Everything depends on the context. We do best to avoid chest-thumping abstractions and general propositions that are appealing but sometimes false. The central question involves the likely effects of particular approaches, whether paternalistic or not. Better understandings of behavioral market failures, and of choice architecture, are uncovering many opportunities for increasing people's welfare without compromising the legitimate claims of freedom of choice. We will uncover many more such opportunities in the future.

Let's take advantage of them. The lives we save may be our own.[1]

Notes

Introduction

1. It is important to emphasize that Mill was concerned with coercion of all kinds, including those forms that come from the private sector and social norms.

2. JOHN STUART MILL, ON LIBERTY 8 (Kathy Casey ed., 2002) (1859).

3. A valuable discussion is DAVID O. BRINK, MILL'S PROGRESSIVE PRINCIPLES (2013).

4. *See* SARAH CONLY, AGAINST AUTONOMY (2012); PATERNALISM: THEORY AND PRACTICE (Christian Coons and Michael Weber eds., 2013).

5. To be sure, the individual mandate can be, and has been, powerfully defended on nonpaternalistic grounds; above all, it should be understood as an effort to overcome a free-rider problem that exists when people do not obtain health insurance (but are nonetheless subsidized in the event that they need medical help).

6. MILL, *supra* note 2.

7. *Id.*

8. *Id.*

9. An authoritative discussion is DANIEL KAHNEMAN, THINKING, FAST AND SLOW (2011). On behavioral economics and public policy, see CASS R. SUNSTEIN, SIMPLER: THE FUTURE OF GOVERNMENT (2013); RICHARD H.

Thaler & Cass R. Sunstein, Nudge: Improving Decisions About Health, Wealth, and Happiness (2008).

10. Richard A. Posner, *Why Is There No Milton Friedman Today*, 10 Econ. J. Watch 210, 212 (2013), *available at* http://econjwatch.org/articles/why-is-there-no-milton-friedman-today-RP.

11. *See* David Laibson, *Golden Eggs and Hyperbolic Discounting*, 112 Q.J. Econ. 443, 445 (1997).

12. For a discussion of some of the foundational issues, see Pedro Bordalo, Nicola Gennaioli & Andrei Shleifer, *Salience Theory of Choice Under Risk*, 127 Q.J. Econ. 1243 (2012); Pedro Bordalo, Nicola Gennaioli & Andrei Shleifer, *Salience in Experimental Tests of the Endowment Effect*, 102 Am. Econ. Rev. 47 (2012).

13. *See* Ted O'Donoghue & Matthew Rabin, *Choice and Procrastination*, 116 Q.J. Econ. 121, 121–22 (2001); Richard H. Thaler & Shlomo Benartzi, *Save More Tomorrow™: Using Behavioral Economics to Increase Employee Saving*, 112 J. Pol. Econ. S164, S168–69 (2004).

14. *See* Eric Johnson & Daniel Goldstein, *Do Defaults Save Lives?*, 302 Science 1338 (2003), *available at* http://papers.ssrn.com/sol3/papers.cfm?abstract_id=1324774; Duncan Watts, Everything Is Obvious 30–31 (2011); Eric Johnson & Daniel Goldstein, *Decisions by Default, in* The Behavioral Foundations of Public Policy 417 (Eldar Shafir ed., 2013).

15. *See* Tali Sharot, The Optimism Bias: A Tour of the Irrationally Positive Brain (2011).

16. *See, e.g.,* Elizabeth W. Dunn, Daniel T. Gilbert & Timothy D. Wilson, *If Money Doesn't Make You Happy, Then You Probably Aren't Spending It Right*, 21 J. Consumer Psychol. 115 (2011); Daniel T. Gilbert et al., *Immune Neglect: A Source of Durability Bias in Affective Forecasting*, 75 J. Personality & Soc. Psychol. 617 (1998).

17. *See* Richard H. Thaler and Will Tucker, *Smarter Information, Smarter Consumers*, Harv. Bus. Rev. January–February, 2012, *available at* http://hbr.org/2013/01/smarter-information-smarter-consumers/ar/pr.

18. *See, e.g.,* http://99u.com/articles/6969/10-Online-Tools-for-Better-Attention-Focus; http://appsforhealthykids.com/; http://exercise.about.com/od/videosmusicsoftware/tp/fitnessapps.htm.

19. For valuable discussion, see Ian Ayres, Carrots and Sticks (2010).

20. *See* Oren Bar-Gill, Seduction by Contract (2012). On the general point, see Andrei Shleifer, *Psychologists at the Gate*, 50 J. Econ. Literature 1080 (2012).

21. *See* Heuristics: The Foundations of Adaptive Behavior (Gerd Gigerenzer et al. eds., 2011).

22. Michael Greenstone, *Toward a Culture of Persistent Regulatory Experimentation and Evaluation, in* New Perspectives on Regulation 111 (David Moss & John Cisternino eds., 2009). For a number of discussions of randomized controlled trials, including nudges, see Abhijit V. Banerjee & Esther Duflo, Poor Economics: A Radical Rethinking of the Way to Fight Global Poverty (2011).

23. *See* Sunstein, *supra* note 9.

24. *See, e.g., id.; see also* Theresa M. Marteau et al., *Changing Human Behavior to Prevent Disease: The Importance of Targeting Automatic Processes,* 337 Science 1492 (2012) (exploring role of automatic processing in behavior in the domain of health).

25. *See The Behavioural Insights Team,* Cabinet Office, http://www .cabinetoffice.gov.uk/behavioural-insights-team (last visited Dec. 10, 2012).

26. *Id.*

27. Various reports can be found at the website of the Behavioural Insights Team. *See id.*

28. *See* Oliver Wright, *Steve Hilton's "Nudge Unit" Goes Global,* Independent (London), Sept. 20, 2012, http://www.independent.co.uk/news/uk/ politics/steve-hiltons-nudge-unit-goes-global-8157492.html.

29. *See Consumer Policy Toolkit,* Org. for Econ. Cooperation & Dev. (July 2010), http://www.oecd.org/sti/consumerpolicy/consumerpolicytool kit.htm.

30. *See* DG SANCO, *Consumer Behaviour: The Road to Effective Policy-Making,* Eur. Commission (2010), http://ec.europa.eu/consumers/docs/ 1dg-sanco-brochure-consumer-behaviour-final.pdf.

31. *See* Sci. for Env't Policy, *Future Brief: Green Behavior,* Eur. Commission (Oct. 2012), http://ec.europa.eu/environment/integration/research/ newsalert/pdf/FB4.pdf. A number of relevant sources can be found at *Resources,* iNudgeYou.com, http://www.inudgeyou.com/resources (last visited Dec. 5, 2012).

32. *See* Changing Behaviours: The Rise of the Psychological State (Rhys Jones et al. eds., 2013).

33. A positive answer is vigorously defended in Sarah Conly, Against Autonomy: Justifying Coercive Paternalism (2012). Negative answers are defended in Riccardo Rebonato, Taking Liberties: A Critical Examination of Libertarian Paternalism (2012); Edward L. Glaeser, *Pater-*

nalism and Psychology, 73 U. Chi. L. Rev. 133 (2006); and Joshua D. Wright
& Douglas H. Ginsburg, *Behavioral Law and Economics: Its Origins, Fatal
Flaws, and Implications for Liberty,* 106 Nw. U. L. Rev. 1033 (2012).

34. *See* Thaler & Sunstein, *supra* note 9, at 252.

35. For one example, see Paul Rozin et al., *Nudge to Nobesity I: Minor
Changes in Accessibility Decrease Food Intake,* 6 Judgment & Decision Making
323, 329 (2011).

36. See Johan Egebark and Mathias Ekström, Can Indifference Make
the World Greener? (2013), available at http://www2.ne.su.se/paper/wp13
_12.pdf

37. David Foster Wallace, *Plain Old Untrendy Troubles and Emotions,* The
Guardian (Sep. 20, 2008), http://www.guardian.co.uk/books/2008/sep/20/
fiction.

38. Amanda Pallais, Small Differences That Matter: Mistakes in Applying to College (2013), available at http://www.nber.org/papers/w19480.

39. It should be emphasized, however, that many behaviorally informed
approaches, such as simplification of complex requirements, need not have
a paternalistic dimension. On choice architecture for choice architects, see
Sunstein, *supra* note 9.

40. *See* Bar-Gill, *supra* note 20, at 2–4.

41. My emphasis here is on behavioral market failures as a supplement
to standard market failures. It is true, of course, that there are other justifications for government action, falling in neither category. We might believe, for example, that prohibitions on discrimination of various kinds, or
protections of privacy, are justified even if there is no behavioral or standard market failure. For one catalogue, see Cass R. Sunstein, After the
Rights Revolution: Reconceiving the Regulatory State 47–73 (1990).

42. *See* Thaler & Sunstein, *supra* note 9, at 8.

43. *See* Brink, *supra* note 3, at 104, suggesting that "shaping choice is
often inescapable, precisely because something has to be the default option.
Why not make the prudentially better option be the default? In this way we
can shape choice so as to produce better prudential outcomes without engaging in paternalistic coercion. . . . It's not clear that Mill's anti-paternalism
should object to shaping choice in this way."

44. Mill, *supra* note 2.

45. Consider, for example, the domains of energy efficiency and fuel
economy, where an analysis of costs and benefits may support stronger

forms of paternalism. On the general topic of coercion, emphasizing the role of costs and benefits, see CONLY, *supra* note 33 (arguing in favor of coercive paternalism). Notably, the interest in nudging and in soft paternalism has been controversial among those who emphasize that mandates and bans may be necessary. *See, e.g., id.;* George Loewenstein & Peter Ubel, Op-Ed, *Economics Behaving Badly*, N.Y. TIMES, July 14, 2010, http://www .nytimes.com/2010/07/15/opinion/15loewenstein.html.

46. *See* BRINK, *supra* note 3, at 176–80, for an excellent discussion.

47. On some of the foundational issues, see MATTHEW ADLER, WELL-BEING AND FAIR DISTRIBUTION: BEYOND COST-BENEFIT ANALYSIS (2011); with respect to paternalism, see CONLY, *supra* note 33, at 7 (suggesting that whether the benefits justify the costs "is the only determinant of acceptability").

48. *See, e.g., id.* at 6–8. The same approach is adopted in CONLY, *supra* note 33, at 11, suggesting that "paternalistic regulations are designed to help us reach our own goals."

49. *See* Anuj K. Shah, Sendhil Mullainathan & Eldar Shafir, *Some Consequences of Having Too Little*, 338 SCIENCE 682 (2012).

50. An especially valuable treatment of these issues is Esther Duflo, Abdul Latif Jameel Professor of Poverty Alleviation & Dev. Econ., Mass. Inst. of Tech., Tanner Lectures on Human Values and the Design of the Fight Against Poverty (May 2, 2012), http://economics.mit.edu/files/7904.

ONE

Occasions for Paternalism

1. *See generally* ADVANCES IN BEHAVIORAL ECONOMICS (Colin F. Camerer et al. eds., 2003) (offering wide range of findings); ADVANCES IN BEHAVIORAL FINANCE, VOLUME II (Richard H. Thaler ed., 2005); CHOICES, VALUES, AND FRAMES (Daniel Kahneman & Amos Tversky eds., 2000) (offering a large number of relevant findings); HEURISTICS AND BIASES: THE PSYCHOLOGY OF INTUITIVE JUDGMENT (Thomas Gilovich et al. eds., 2002) (outlining a variety of empirical findings).

2. DANIEL KAHNEMAN, THINKING, FAST AND SLOW (2011); *see also* RICHARD H. THALER & CASS R. SUNSTEIN, NUDGE: IMPROVING DECISIONS ABOUT HEALTH, WEALTH, AND HAPPINESS 19–22 (2008) (discussing "Humans" and "Econs").

3. *See* Thaler & Sunstein, *supra* note 2.

4. Colin Camerer et al., *Neuroeconomics: How Neuroscience Can Inform Economics*, 43 J. Econ. Literature 1, 17 (2005).

5. *See* The Human Amygdala (Paul J. Whalen & Elizabeth A. Phelps eds., 2009).

6. *See* Jason P. Mitchell et al., *Medial Prefrontal Cortex Predicts Intertemporal Choice*, 23 J. Cognitive Neurosci. 1, 6 (2010).

7. *Id.*

8. For a valuable and important study, see Tatiana A. Homonoff, "Can Small Incentives Have Large Effects? The Impact of Taxes Versus Bonuses on Small Bag Use" (job market paper, Princeton University, Princeton, NJ, October 26, 2012), www.princeton.edu/~homonoff/THomonoff_Job MarketPaper.

9. Boaz Keysar, Sayuri L. Hayakawa & Sun Gyu An, *The Foreign-Language Effect: Thinking in a Foreign Tongue Reduces Decision Biases*, 23 Psychol. Sci. 661 (2012).

10. *Id.* at 666–67.

11. Beckett said that the French language had an "aura of unfamiliarity about it," and that it allowed him to "escape the habits inherent in the use of a native language." The Grove Companion to Samuel Beckett: A Reader's Guide to His Works, Life, and Thought 206 (C. J. Ackerly & S. E. Gontarski eds., 2004).

12. *See, e.g.*, W. Kip Viscusi, Rational Risk Policy (1998).

13. *See* The Feeling of Risk: New Perspectives on Risk Perception 3–20 (Paul Slovic ed., 2010).

14. *See* Jonathan Haidt, The Righteous Mind (2012) (arguing that many judgments are automatic and intuitive, and how our deliberative system works hard to justify those judgments ex post).

15. *See* Kahneman, *supra* note 2, at 97–99.

16. For a related finding in the political domain, testifying to the power of System 1, see Christopher H. Achen & Larry M. Bartels, *Blind Retrospection: Electoral Responses to Drought, Flu, and Shark Attacks* (Working Paper No. 199/2004, 2004), http://www.march.es/ceacs/publicaciones/working/archivos/2004_199.pdf.

17. John Stuart Mill, On Liberty 8 (Kathy Casey ed., 2002) (1859).

18. *See* David O. Brink, Mill's Progressive Principles (2013) for instructive discussion.

19. *See, e.g.*, Hunt Allcott, Sendhil Mullainathan & Dmitry Taubinsky, *Energy Policy with Externalities and Internalities* (Nat'l Bureau of Econ. Research, Working Paper No. 17,977, 2012), http://www.nber.org/papers/w17977 (explaining that people often do not consider the long-term effects of energy efficiency and how policies might help them to do so, thus combating "internalities").

20. *See* Ted O'Donoghue & Matthew Rabin, *Choice and Procrastination*, 116 Q.J. Econ. 121, 121–22 (2001); Richard H. Thaler & Shlomo Benartzi, *Save More Tomorrow™: Using Behavioral Economics to Increase Employee Saving*, 112 J. Pol. Econ. S164, S168–69 (2004). In the context of poverty, see Abhijit Banerjee & Esther Duflo, Poor Economics: A Radical Rethinking of the Way To Fight Global Poverty 64–68 (2011). For an important, relevant discussion that involves not procrastination but cognitive load, see Anuj K. Shah, Sendhil Mullainathan & Elda Shafir, *Some Consequences of Having Too Little*, 338 Science 682 (2012). On that general theme, see Sendhil Mullainathan & Eldar Shafir, Scarcity: Why Having Too Little Means So Much (2013).

21. *See, e.g.*, Jess Benhabib, Alberto Bisin & Andrew Schotter, *Present-Bias, Quasi-Hyperbolic Discounting, and Fixed Costs*, 69 Games & Econ. Behav. 205 (2010).

22. *Cf.* Dean Karlan et al., *Getting to the Top of Mind: How Reminders Increase Saving* 1, 14 (Yale Econ. Dept., Working Paper No. 82, 2010), http://karlan.yale.edu/p/Top-of-Mind-April2010.pdf (showing value of reminders in getting people to attend to savings).

23. *See* Esther Duflo, Michael Kremer & Jonathan Robinson, *Nudging Farmers to Use Fertilizer: Evidence from Kenya*, 101 Am. Econ. Review 2350, 2351–54 (2011) (finding that farmers in western Kenya do not make economically advantageous fertilizer investments, but that a small, time-limited discount on the cost of fertilizer can increase investments, thus producing higher welfare than either a laissez-faire approach or large subsidies).

24. *See* Eric Johnson & Daniel Goldstein, *Decisions by Default, in* The Behavioral Foundations of Public Policy 417 (Eldar Shafir ed., 2013); Cass R. Sunstein, *Impersonal Default Rules vs. Active Choices vs. Personalized Default Rules: A Triptych* (SSRN Elec. Library, Working Paper No. 2,171,343, 2012), http://ssrn.com/abstract=2171343. An important discussion, with many implications, is Raj Chetty et al., Active vs. Passive Decisions and Crowdout in

Retirement Savings Accounts: Evidence from Denmark, available at http://obs.rc.fas.harvard.edu/chetty/crowdout.pdf.

25. *See* David Laibson, *Golden Eggs and Hyperbolic Discounting,* 112 Q.J. Econ. 443, 445 (1997).

26. *See* Richard H. Thaler & H. M. Shefrin, *An Economic Theory of Self-Control,* 89 J. Pol. Econ. 392, 404 (1981). For an interesting application, discussed in more detail below, see Jonathan H. Gruber & Sendhil Mullainathan, *Do Cigarette Taxes Make Smokers Happier?,* 5 Advances Econ. Analysis & Pol'y 1, 20 (2005).

27. *See* Haiyan Shui & Lawrence M. Ausubel, *Time Inconsistency in the Credit Card Market* (SSRN Elec. Library, Working Paper No. 586,622, 2004), http://ssrn.com/abstract=586622. For a technical treatment, see Roland Benabou & Marek Pycia, *Dynamic Inconsistency and Self-Control: A Planner-Doer Interpretation,* 77 Econ. Letters 419 (2002).

28. *See* Mitchell et al., *supra* note 6, at 4–5.

29. *Id.* at 1.

30. *Id.* at 5.

31. *Id.* at 6.

32. *See, e.g.,* Jonathan Gruber, *Smoking's "Internalities,"* Reg., 25(4) Winter 2002–2003, at 52; Richard Herrnstein et al., *Utility Maximization and Melioration: Internalities in Individual Choice,* 6 J. Behav. Decision Making 149 (1993); Allcott et al., *supra* note 19.

33. *See* Ian Ayres, Carrots and Sticks 47 (2010).

34. Allcott et al., *supra* note 19, at 31, 35.

35. *See* Allcott et al., *supra* note 19, at 2–3, 9–10; Hunt Allcott & Nathan Wozny, *Gasoline Prices, Fuel Economy, and the Energy Paradox* (Nat'l Bureau of Econ. Research, Working Paper No. 18,583, 2012), http://www.nber.org/papers/w18583.

36. This is the basic argument of Sarah Conly, Against Autonomy: Justifying Coercive Paternalism (2012), who emphasizes the need to assess the full set of costs and benefits.

37. *See* Christopher Chabris & Daniel Simons, The Invisible Gorilla: And Other Ways Our Intuitions Deceive Us 6–8 (2010).

38. *See* Oren Bar-Gill, Seduction by Contract 18–23 (2012). Early work by Daniel Kahneman focused on closely related questions. *See* Daniel Kahneman, Attention and Effort (1973).

39. *See* Victor Stango & Jonathan Zinman, *Limited and Varying Consumer Attention: Evidence from Shocks to the Salience of Bank Overdraft Fees* 27–28

(Fed. Reserve Bank of Phila., Working Paper No. 11-17, 2011), http://ssrn
.com/ abstract=1817916.

40. *Id.* at 25, 27.

41. *See* Alix Peterson Zwane et al., *Being Surveyed Can Change Later
Behavior and Related Parameter Estimates,* 108 PROC. NAT'L ACAD. SCI. 1821,
1825–26 (2011).

42. *See* Ximena Cadena & Antoinette Schoar, *Remembering to Pay? Reminders vs. Financial Incentives for Loan Payments* (Nat'l Bureau of Econ. Research, Working Paper No. 17020, 2011), http://www.nber.org/papers/
w17020. Checklists work for similar reasons. *See* MARTY MAKARY, UN-
ACCOUNTABLE: WHAT HOSPITALS WON'T TELL YOU AND HOW TRANSPARENCY
CAN REVOLUTIONIZE HEALTH CARE (2012).

43. *See* Steffen Altman & Christian Traxler, *Nudges at the Dentist* (Inst.
for the Study of Labor, Discussion Paper No. 6699, 2012), http://ftp.iza
.org/dp6699.pdf.

44. *See* Behavioural Insights Unit, *Applying Behavioral Insights to Charitable Giving* (2013), available at https://www.gov.uk/government/uploads/
system/uploads/attachment_data/file/203286/BIT_Charitable_Giving
_Paper.pdf.

45. *See* Xavier Gabaix & David Laibson, *Shrouded Attributes, Consumer
Myopia, and Information Suppression in Competitive Markets,* 121 Q.J. ECON.
505, 511 (2006).

46. *See* Cass R. Sunstein, *Empirically Informed Regulation,* 78 U. CHI. L.
REV. 1349, 1373 (2011).

47. *See* NAT'L HIGHWAY TRAFFIC ADMIN., DEP'T OF TRANSP., Final Regulatory Impact Analysis: Corporate Average Fuel Economy for MY2017–MY
2025 Passenger Cars and Light Trucks (2012).

48. *Id.* at 983 (internal citations omitted). For a valuable overview, showing the complexity of the underlying issues and the amount that remains
to be learned, see Hunt Allcott & Michael Greenstone, *Is There an Energy
Efficiency Gap?,* 26 J. ECON. PERSP. 3 (2012). For an important discussion of
externalities and internalities, see Allcott et al., *supra* note 19.

49. In the same spirit, see CONLY, *supra* note 36, at 6–12. I do not explore here the question whether fuel-economy standards are the ideal tool
or whether other options would be preferable. For relevant discussion, see
Allcott et al., *supra* note 19; on the underlying questions, see Allcott &
Wozny, *supra* note 35.

50. *See* TALI SHAROT, THE OPTIMISM BIAS: A TOUR OF THE IRRATIONALLY

POSITIVE BRAIN (2011) (discussing unrealistic optimism, with particular reference to neurological foundations); Tali Sharot et al., *How Unrealistic Optimism Is Maintained in the Face of Reality*, 14 NATURE NEUROSCIENCE 1475 (2011) (showing that people do not update when receiving bad information as well as they do when receiving good information). *See also* Christine Jolls, *Behavioral Economics Analysis of Redistributive Legal Rules*, 51 VAND. L. REV. 1653, 1659 (1998).

51. *See generally* SHAROT, *supra* note 50 (explaining nature and sources of skew toward unrealistic optimism); TALI SHAROT, THE SCIENCE OF OPTIMISM: WHY WE'RE HARD-WIRED FOR HOPE (2012).

52. Tali Sharot et al., *Selectively Altering Belief Formation in the Human Brain*, 109 PROC. NAT'L ACAD. SCI. 17058 (2012), http://www.pnas.org/cgi/doi/10.1073/pnas.1205828109.

53. *See* BAR-GILL, *supra* note 38, at 21–26.

54. *See* Christine Jolls & Cass R. Sunstein, *Debiasing Through Law*, 35 J. LEGAL STUD. 199, 215 (2006).

55. *See* SHAROT, *supra* note 50, at x–xiv.

56. *See* Neil D. Weinstein, *Unrealistic Optimism About Susceptibility to Health Problems: Conclusions from a Community-Wide Sample*, 10 J. BEHAV. MED. 481, 494–96 (1987). For an interesting complication, showing that people sometimes tend to see themselves as below-average for difficult or unusual tasks, see Don A. Moore & Deborah A. Small, *Error and Bias in Comparative Judgment: On Being Both Better and Worse than We Think We Are*, 92 J. PERSONALITY & SOC. PSYCHOL. 972 (2007).

57. *See* Paul Slovic, *Do Adolescent Smokers Know the Risks?*, 47 DUKE L.J. 1133, 1136–37 (1998).

58. *See* David Eil & Justin M. Rao, *The Good News–Bad News Effect: Asymmetrical Processing of Objective Information About Yourself*, 3 AM. ECON. J. MICROECON. 114, 116–17 (2011).

59. *See* SHAROT ET AL., *supra* note 50.

60. *Id.* at 1477. For some compelling evidence of the neural foundations of optimism, and particularly the more ready incorporation of good news than bad news, see SHAROT ET AL., *supra* note 52.

61. SHAROT ET AL., *supra* note 50, at 1477.

62. *See id.*

63. *See* Amos Tversky & Daniel Kahneman, *Availability: A Heuristic for Judging Frequency and Probability*, 5 COGNITIVE PSYCHOL. 207, 221 (1973).

64. *See* Elke U. Weber, *Experience-Based and Description-Based Perceptions*

of Long-Term Risk: Why Global Warming Does Not Scare Us (Yet), 77 CLI-MATIC CHANGE 103, 107–8 (2006).

65. *See* Laurette Dubé-Rioux & J. Edward Russo, *An Availability Bias in Professional Judgment*, 1 J. BEHAV. DECISION MAKING 223, 233–34 (1988); Paul Slovic, Baruch Fischhoff & Sarah Lichtenstein, *Cognitive Processes and Societal Risk Taking, in* THE PERCEPTION OF RISK 37–38 (Paul Slovic ed., 2000).

66. *See* George F. Loewenstein et al., *Risk as Feelings*, 127 PSYCHOL. BULL. 267, 280 (2001); Cass R. Sunstein, *Probability Neglect: Emotions, Worst Cases, and Law*, 112 YALE L.J. 61 (2002).

67. *See* Yuval Rottenstreich & Christopher K. Hsee, *Money, Kisses, and Electric Shocks: On the Affective Psychology of Risk*, 12 PSYCHOL. SCI. 185, 185 (2001). For a demonstration that probability is often neglected with respect to things, but not with respect to money (without, however, emphasizing the role of emotions), see A. Peter McGraw, Eldar Shafir & Alexander Todorov, *Valuing Money and Things: Why a $20 Item Can Be Worth More and Less than $20*, 56 MGMT. SCI. 816, 827 (2010). For a discussion of emotions and risk, see generally THE FEELING OF RISK: NEW PERSPECTIVES ON RISK PERCEPTION (Paul Slovic ed., 2010).

T W O

The Paternalist's Toolbox

1. There are important questions, not explored here, about the grounds for distinguishing between paternalism from government and paternalism from nongovernmental actors. One obvious ground involves coercion, but (as discussed in detail below) some forms of government paternalism are not coercive, and some forms of private paternalism can be understood as coercive (as, for example, when an employer threatens an employee with discharge if he or she does not manage a self-control problem that does not affect others). And while I cannot discuss the complexities here, it is reasonable to think that some of the findings discussed here provide new support for paternalistic steps—at least nudges—from those with expertise, including doctors.

2. *See, e.g.*, Kevin Loria, *New York Soda Ban Proposal: Public Hearing Gets Impassioned*, CHRISTIAN SCI. MONITOR, July 24, 2012, http://www.csmonitor .com/USA/Society/2012/0724/New-York-soda-ban-proposal-Public -hearing-gets-impassioned.

3. JOHN STUART MILL, ON LIBERTY 8 (Kathy Casey ed., 2002) (1859).

4. For a valuable and relevant discussion, bearing particularly on means paternalism, see B. Douglas Bernheim & Antonio Rangel, *Beyond Revealed Preference: Choice Theoretic Foundations for Behavioral Welfare Economics*, 124 Q.J. Econ. 51 (2009).

5. It is possible, of course, that a fine could affect beliefs, not just actions. For example, a fine could convey information about the appropriate attitude to have toward an activity or a product, and that information could influence beliefs.

6. To be sure, it might affect people's beliefs (for example, by making people think that the risks are very serious), and influence their behavior for that reason.

7. *See* Robert A. Kagan & Jerome H. Skolnick, *Banning Smoking: Compliance Without Enforcement, in* Smoking Policy: Law, Politics, and Culture 69, 72 (Robert L. Rabin & Stephen D. Sugarman eds., 1993) (finding high compliance in part because of expressive function of law).

8. *See* Tatiana A. Homonoff, "Can Small Incentives Have Large Effects? The Impact of Taxes Versus Bonuses on Disposable Bag Use" (job market paper, Princeton University, Princeton, NJ, October 26, 2012), http://www.princeton.edu/~homonoff/THomonoff_JobMarketPaper.

9. Riccardo Rebonato, Taking Liberties: A Critical Examination of Libertarian Paternalism (2012).

10. *See* Lawrence Lessig, *The Regulation of Social Meaning*, 62 U. Chi. L. Rev. 943 (1995).

11. Mill, *supra* note 3.

12. *See* Sunit Agarwal et al., Regulating Consumer Financial Products: Evidence from Credit Cards (2013), available at http://www.nber.org/papers/w19484.

13. *See* Sarah Conly, Against Autonomy: Justifying Coercive Paternalism 149–80 (2012).

14. *See* Cass R. Sunstein, *Empirically Informed Regulation*, 78 U. Chi. L. Rev. 1349, 1373 (2011).

15. *See id.*

16. I am bracketing here any questions about personal identity over time. *See generally* Derek Parfit, Reasons and Persons (1984) (exploring those questions in detail).

17. *See* Conly, *supra* note 12, at 1–16, for the plausible suggestion that some cases are really not so difficult by this measure.

18. Mill, *supra* note 3.

19. *See* Conly, *supra* note 12, for instructive discussion.

20. John Stuart Mill, Utilitarianism (1861).

21. See the treatment of perfectionism in Conly, *supra* note 12, at 100–125.

22. *See* Brian Wansink, Mindless Eating (2010); Brian Wansink, Slim By Design: Mindless Eating Solutions for Everyday Life (forthcoming 2014).

23. It is possible, however, that paternalistic justifications could be offered for these laws, involving the effects of discrimination on choosers. There is also a possibility of autopaternalism, as, for example, when people seek to bind themselves, perhaps through law. *See* Jon Elster, Ulysses and the Sirens: Studies in Rationality and Irrationality (1984). With the exception of a few brief remarks, I do not explore autopaternalism here, though it does have an obvious relationship to some responses to behavioral market failures from which people might be attempting to protect themselves.

24. In the same general vein, see Conly, *supra* note 12, at 1–15. Note, however, that Conly argues in favor of coercive (or "hard") forms of paternalism, which I treat very cautiously here. We do agree that the master concept involves an assessment of costs and benefits (including the frustration felt by those whose choices are influenced by paternalists).

25. *See Tips from Former Smokers*, Ctrs. for Disease Control & Prevention, http://www.cdc.gov/tobacco/campaign/tips/resources/videos (last updated Nov. 28, 2012).

26. *See* Required Warnings for Cigarette Packages and Advertisements, 76 Fed. Reg. 36,628 (June 22, 2011) (to be codified at 21 C.F.R. pt. 1141). The rule was invalidated in *R. J. Reynolds Tobacco Co. v. FDA*, 696 F.3d 1205 (D.C. Cir. 2012), but upheld in *Discount Tobacco City & Lottery, Inc. v. United States*, 674 F.3d 509 (6th Cir. 2012).

27. Michael Howard Saul, *Mayor's Soda Plan Fails*, Wall St. J., Aug. 20, 2011, http://online.wsj.com/article/SB10001424053111903596904576518902332775160.html.

28. For example, an effect might be framed as a gain or as a loss. For an excellent collection, see Perspectives on Framing (Gideon Keren ed., 2010).

29. *See R. J. Reynolds Tobacco Co. v. FDA*, 845 F. Supp. 2d 266, 272 (D.D.C. 2012).

THREE
Paternalism and Welfare

1. *See* OREN BAR-GILL, SEDUCTION BY CONTRACT 26–32 (2012) (exploring the extent to which market pressures may encourage exploitation of behavioral biases).

2. JOHN STUART MILL, ON LIBERTY 8 (Kathy Casey ed., 2002) (1859).

3. *See* F. A. Hayek, *The Use of Knowledge in Society*, 35 AM. ECON. REV. 519, 524–26 (1945).

4. MILL, *supra* note 2.

5. *See, e.g.*, Gabriel D. Carroll et al., *Optimal Defaults and Active Decisions*, 124 Q.J. ECON. 1639 (2009). For a vigorous suggestion that soft paternalism will impede learning, see Joshua D. Wright & Douglas H. Ginsburg, *Behavioral Law and Economics: Its Origins, Fatal Flaws, and Implications for Liberty*, 106 Nw. U. L. REV. 1033 (2012); on the underlying issues, see Bruce Ian Carlin et al., Libertarian Paternalism, Information Production, and Financial Decision-Making (June 6, 2012) (unpublished manuscript), http://faculty.fuqua.duke.edu/~sgervais/Research/Papers/Libertarian Paternalism.WP.pdf.

6. MILL, *supra* note 2.

7. *Id.*

8. *Id.*

9. *Id.*

10. *See* JOHN STUART MILL, UTILITARIANISM (1861), for a version of this argument. Related discussion can be found in Edward L. Glaeser, *Paternalism and Psychology*, 73 U. CHI. L. REV. 133 135–42 (2006), which emphasizes the ability of those in the private sector to balance relevant values and to incorporate new information.

11. MILL, *supra* note 2.

12. *Id.*

13. *See* Cass R. Sunstein, *Impersonal Default Rules vs. Active Choices vs. Personalized Default Rules: A Triptych* (SSRN Elec. Library, Working Paper No. 2,171,343, 2012), http://ssrn.com/abstract=2171343, at 21–24.

14. *See, e.g.*, GORDON TULLOCK, ARTHUR SELDON & GORDON LO BRADY, GOVERNMENT FAILURE: A PRIMER IN PUBLIC CHOICE (2002).

15. *See* Timur Kuran & Cass R. Sunstein, *Availability Cascades and Risk Regulation*, 51 STAN. L. REV. 683 (1999). The point regarding the shortcomings of behavioral economics is emphasized in Wright & Ginsburg, *supra* note 5.

16. *See* Glaeser, *supra* note 10, for arguments in this vein; Wright & Ginsburg, *supra* note 5; Niclas Berggren, *Time for Behavioral Political Economy? An Analysis of Articles in Behavioral Economics* (The Ratio Institute, Ratio Working Paper No. 166, 2011), http://www.ratio.se/media/81477/nb _behavioral.pdf.

17. For a general discussion, see Cass R. Sunstein, *The Office of Information and Regulatory Affairs: Myths and Realities*, 126 Harv. L. Rev. 1838 (2013).

18. *See* Cass R. Sunstein, *Cognition and Cost-Benefit Analysis*, 29 J. Legal. Stud. 1059 (2000); Sunstein, *supra* note 17.

19. *See* Kuran & Sunstein, *supra* note 15.

20. *See* Mill, *supra* note 2.

21. *See* Jonathan Haidt, The Righteous Mind (2012).

22. See the discussion of perfectionism in Sarah Conly, Against Autonomy: Justifying Coercive Paternalism 100–125 (2012). I do not much discuss here the strand in Mill that emphasizes the importance of "experiments in living." *See* Elizabeth S. Anderson, *John Stuart Mill and Experiments in Living*, 102 Ethics 4 (1991). Appropriate responses to behavioral market failures of the kind outlined here would not seem to run afoul of Mill's emphasis on such experiments. To be sure, some actions that appear to demonstrate self-control problems might be seen as experiments in living, but disclosure requirements and warnings allow such experiments to continue. It is hard to see how fuel-economy requirements or energy-efficiency mandates plausibly jeopardize experiments in living, even though these are hard forms of paternalism.

23. Mill, *supra* note 2.

24. *See, e.g.*, Daniel Kahneman, Thinking, Fast and Slow (2011); Elizabeth W. Dunn, Daniel T. Gilbert & Timothy D. Wilson, *If Money Doesn't Make You Happy, Then You Probably Aren't Spending It Right*, 21 J. Consumer Psychol. 115, 115 (2011). For some important cautionary notes about the ability of even close friends to know what people will like, see Joel Waldfogel, Scroogenomics: Why You Shouldn't Buy Presents for the Holidays (2009). It is possible to agree with Waldfogel's basic claims while also accepting the existence of behavioral market failures.

25. Daniel J. Benjamin et al., *What Do You Think Would Make You Happier? What Do You Think You Would Choose?*, 102 Am. Econ. Rev. 2083, 2085–86 (2012).

26. *See* Niklas Karlsson, George Loewenstein & Jane McCafferty, *The*

Economics of Meaning, 30 Nordic J. Pol. Econ. 61, 62 (2004); Peter A. Ubel & George Loewenstein, *Pain and Suffering Awards: They Shouldn't Be (Just) About Pain and Suffering*, 37 J. Legal Stud. S195, S206–7 (2008).

27. Benjamin et al., *supra* note 25, at 2085.

28. *See* Daniel T. Gilbert et al., *Immune Neglect: A Source of Durability Bias in Affective Forecasting*, 75 J. Personality & Soc. Psychol. 617, 618 (1998).

29. *See* Waldfogel, *supra* note 24.

30. *See* Jonathan H. Gruber & Sendhil Mullainathan, *Do Cigarette Taxes Make Smokers Happier?*, 5 Advances Econ. Analysis & Pol'y 1, 2 (2005).

31. *See, e.g.*, Lucia Reisch & Wencke Gwozdz, Smart Defaults and Soft Nudges: How Insights from Behavioral Economics Can Inform Effective Nutrition Policy (unpublished manuscript 2012) (discussing the uses and limits of nudges and outlining and apparently approving of steps in Denmark, Hungary, and France to tax certain foods); Jeff Strnad, *Conceptualizing the "Fat Tax": The Role of Food Taxes in Developed Economies* (John M. Olin Program in Law & Econ., Working Paper No. 286, 2004), http://ssrn.com/abstract=561321.

32. *See* Christopher Snowden, The Proof of the Pudding: Denmark's Fat Tax Fiasco (2013), available at http://www.iea.org.uk/publications/research/the-proof-of-the-pudding-denmark's-fat-tax-fiasco.

33. *See* Glaeser, *supra* note 10; Wright & Ginsburg, *supra* note 5.

34. *See* Glaeser, *supra* note 10, which has a rule-consequentialist flavor, but which is qualified through a recognition that (optional) nudging is justified in identifiable cases.

35. Mill, *supra* note 2.

36. For a valuable discussion, see Edna Ullmann-Margalit, *Invisible Hand Explanations*, 39 Synthese 263 (1978).

37. For discussion, see Richard H. Thaler & Cass R. Sunstein, Nudge: Improving Decisions About Health, Wealth, and Happiness (2008). Richard Thaler et al., *Choice Architecture*, in Behavioral Foundations of Policy 428, 428–31 (Eldar Shafir ed. 2012). I am bracketing here the potential effects of the kinds of choice architecture that are established by the basic rules of contract law, property law, tort law, and criminal law.

38. *See* Cass R. Sunstein, Simpler: The Future of Government (2013).

39. *See* Exec. Order No. 13,563, 76 Fed. Reg. 3821 (Jan. 21, 2011) (directing agencies to catalogue costs and benefits and to ensure, to the extent permitted by law, that the benefits justify the costs); Sunstein, *supra* note 17.

40. James Madison, Notes of Debates in the Federal Convention of 1787, at 83 (Adrienne Koch ed., 1984) (statement of James Madison).

41. For one account, see *Senate Legislative Process*, United States Senate, http://www.senate.gov/legislative/common/briefing/Senate_legislative _process.htm (last visited Dec. 5, 2012).

FOUR

Paternalism and Autonomy

1. *See* Riccardo Rebonato, Taking Liberties: A Critical Examination of Libertarian Paternalism (2012); Joshua D. Wright & Douglas H. Ginsburg, *Behavioral Law and Economics: Its Origins, Fatal Flaws, and Implications for Liberty*, 106 Nw. U. L. Rev. 1033 (2012). Sarah Conly, Against Autonomy: Justifying Coercive Paternalism (2012), discusses and rejects the objection from respect; *see, e.g.*, pp. 33–40.

2. For relevant discussion, see J. S. Blumenthal-Barby & Hadley Burroughs, *Seeking Better Health Care Outcomes: The Ethics of Using the "Nudge,"* 12 Am. J. Bioethics 1 (2012).

3. *See* Bjorn Bartling et al., The Intrinsic Value of Decision Rights (2013), available at http://papers.ssrn.com/sol3/papers.cfm?abstract_id= 2274618.

4. *See* Sheena Iyengar, The Art of Choosing (2010); Conly, *supra* note 1, at 90–94.

5. Those who emphasize autonomy tend to allow override when compelling reason exists. For an overview, see Larry Alexander, *Deontology at the Threshold*, 37 San Diego L. Rev. 893, 898–901 (2000). For an emphasis on the importance of autonomy, see Wright & Ginsburg, *supra* note 1.

6. *See* Gidon Felsen et al., *Decisional Enhancement and Autonomy: Public Attitudes Toward Overt and Covert Nudges*, 8 Judgment and Decision Making 202 (2013).

7. Peter B. Reiner, *Are You Willing to Be Nudged into Making the Right Decision*, Slate (Aug. 13, 2013) (emphasis in original), available at http:// www.slate.com/blogs/future_tense/2013/08/13/research_shows_when _nudging_works_and_when_it_doesn_t.html.

8. Susan Parker, *Esther Duflo Explains Why She Believes Randomized Controlled Trials Are So Vital*, The Center for Effective Philanthropy Blog (June 23, 2011), http://www.effectivephilanthropy.org/blog/2011/06/ esther-duflo-explains-why-she-believes-randomized-controlled-trials-are

-so-vital. Duflo develops these ideas in detail in her 2012 Tanner Lectures. *See* Esther Duflo, Abdul Latif Jameel Professor of Poverty Alleviation & Dev. Econ., Mass. Inst. of Tech., Tanner Lectures on Human Values and the Design of the Fight Against Poverty (May 2, 2012), http://economics.mit .edu/files/7904. A relevant and valuable discussion is ABHIJIT BANERJEE & ESTHER DUFLO, POOR ECONOMICS: A RADICAL RETHINKING OF THE WAY TO FIGHT GLOBAL POVERTY (2011).

   9. A view of this sort is defended and elaborated by Joshua Greene. *See, e.g.*, Joshua D. Greene, *The Cognitive Neuroscience of Moral Judgment, in* THE COGNITIVE NEUROSCIENCES 987 (Michael S. Gazzaniga ed., 4th ed. 2009); Joshua D. Greene et al., *Cognitive Load Selectively Interferes with Utilitarian Moral Judgment,* 107 COGNITION 1144 (2008). The latter paper states: "[O]ur theory associates utilitarian moral judgment (approving of harmful actions that maximize good consequences) with controlled cognitive processes and associates non-utilitarian moral judgment with automatic emotional responses. Consistent with this theory, we find that a cognitive load manipulation selectively interferes with utilitarian judgment. This interference effect provides direct evidence for the influence of controlled cognitive processes in moral judgment, and utilitarian moral judgment more specifically." *Id.* at 1144.

   10. *Id.; see* Joshua D. Greene, *Why Are VMPFC Patients More Utilitarian? A Dual-Process Theory of Moral Judgment Explains,* 11 TRENDS IN COGNITIVE SCI. 322 (2007); Cass R. Sunstein, *Moral Heuristics,* 28 BEHAV. & BRAIN SCI. 531 (2005); Cass R. Sunstein, Is Deontology A Heuristic? On Psychology, Neuroscience, Ethics, and Law (unpublished manuscript 2013), available at http://papers.ssrn.com/sol3/papers.cfm?abstract_id=2304760.

   11. HENRY SIDGWICK, THE METHODS OF ETHICS 425–26 (7th ed. 1981).

   12. I am noting this possibility, but I am not aware of any evidence to support it.

   13. *See, e.g.*, F. M. KAMM, INTRICATE ETHICS: RIGHTS, RESPONSIBILITIES, AND PERMISSIBLE HARM (2007).

   14. For relevant discussion, see 1 DEREK PARFIT, ON WHAT MATTERS (2011).

   15. *See supra* note 9.

   16. *See* Duflo, *supra* note 8; CONLY, *supra* note 1, at 90 ("I hate the time that self-regulation takes from things that I actually am interested in. . . . While some people write as if every time a freedom were taken from us we kick and scream and feel deprived, others, more realistic, recognize that

the responsibility for making such choices is a burden, and one that we are often quite willing to give up"); Sendhil Mullainathan & Eldar Shafir, Scarcity: Why Having Too Little Means So Much (2012).

17. *See* Cass R. Sunstein, *Empirically Informed Regulation*, 78 U. Chi. L. Rev. 1349, 1373 (2011).

18. For discussion of the energy paradox, see Adam B. Jaffe & Robert N. Stavins, *The Energy Paradox and the Diffusion of Conservation Technology*, 16 Resource & Energy Econ. 91, 92–94 (1994). For a helpful and somewhat skeptical discussion, see Hunt Allcott & Michael Greenstone, *Is There an Energy Efficiency Gap?*, 26 J. Econ. Persp. 3 (2012). It is clear that more research is needed on this topic.

<h3 style="text-align:center">FIVE
Soft Paternalism and Its Discontents</h3>

1. *See Ry. Express Agency v. New York*, 336 U.S. 106, 112–13 (1949) (Jackson, J., concurring).

2. *Id.*

3. F. A. von Hayek, The Constitution of Liberty 155 (1960).

4. *See* Edward L. Glaeser, *Paternalism and Psychology*, 73 U. Chi. L. Rev. 133, 149 (2006).

5. *See* Sarah Conly, Against Autonomy: Justifying Coercive Paternalism 7–8 (2012), for the suggestion that nudging can be both manipulative and ineffective, thus giving us "the worst of both worlds."

6. *See* Glaeser, *supra* note 4, at 151.

7. For an interesting discussion of public reactions to overt and covert nudges, see Gidon Felsen et al., *Decisional Enhancement and Autonomy: Public Attitudes Toward Overt and Covert Nudges*, 8 Judgment and Decision Making 202 (2013).

8. For a valuable study of the difference between overt and covert nudges, see *id.*

9. *See id.*

10. *See* John Beshears et al., The Limitations of Defaults 8 (unpublished manuscript, 2010), http://www.nber.org/programs/ag/rrc/NB10-02,%20Beshears,%20Choi,%20Laibson,%20Madrian.pdf. *See also* Zachary Brown et al., *Testing the Effects of Defaults on the Thermostat Settings of OECD Employees*, 39 Energy Economics 128 (2013), which finds that in winter, OECD employees were often willing to change back a significant (two-degree C)

reduction in the default thermostat setting—but that they were less likely to change a smaller reduction (one-degree C).

11. *See* RICCARDO REBONATO, TAKING LIBERTIES: A CRITICAL EXAMINA- TION OF LIBERTARIAN PATERNALISM (2012).

12. JOHN STUART MILL, ON LIBERTY 8 (Kathy Casey ed., 2002) (1859).

13. ANTONIO R. DAMASIO, DESCARTES' ERROR: EMOTION, REASON AND THE HUMAN BRAIN 37, 193–94 (2008).

14. *Id.* at 193–94.

15. *See* CONLY, *supra* note 5, at 103–11, for a discussion of paternalism and perfectionism. Conly supports hard paternalism, but only as a means of promoting people's own ends, and not in order to displace them. She rejects perfectionism. The paternalism defended here is similarly focused on means, not ends (with the qualifications I have explored); my discussion is thus compatible with Conly's rejection of perfectionism.

Epilogue

1. With apologies and gratitude to the great Flannery O'Connor and the great Thomas Schelling, each of whom used a similar phrase in a quite different context. *See The Life You Save May Be Your Own, in* FLANNERY O'CONNOR, THE COMPLETE STORIES (1971); *The Life You Save May Be Your Own, in* THOMAS SCHELLING, CHOICE AND CONSEQUENCE (1984).

Acknowledgments

This book is a revised version of the Storrs Lectures in Jurisprudence, which were given at Yale Law School on November 12 and 13, 2012. Special thanks to Dean Robert Post and the Yale Law School faculty for the great honor of inviting me to give those lectures. Thanks also to audiences at Yale Law School for their graciousness and kindness, and for a host of valuable thoughts and suggestions. The book is much better because of their help.

I am grateful as well to many colleagues and friends for their comments and ideas, including Bruce Ackerman, Esther Duflo, Elizabeth Emens, Christine Jolls, Martha Nussbaum, Eric Posner, Richard Posner, Lucia Reisch, and Adrian Vermeule. Daniel Kanter provided excellent comments and research assistance. Duflo's work on paternalism, which can be found in her 2012 Tanner Lectures, was a great help throughout. The manuscript was much improved as a result of an excellent reader's report from Sarah Conly and a host of suggestions from participants in superb workshops at Harvard's Department of Economics, Harvard's Kennedy School of Government, and the University of Chicago Booth School of Business. At the final stages, Talia Gillis provided superb research assistance.

I owe a particular debt to Richard Thaler for comments and for many years of discussion of these topics. Thaler does not agree with everything said here (though I hope eventually to convince him), and hence nothing in this book should be taken as reflective of a shared view about nudges and paternalism.

Special thanks are due to William Frucht for terrific editing and for wise counsel on matters large and small. Special thanks as well to my agent, Sarah Chalfant, for sage advice on the project. I am grateful to my amazing wife, Samantha Power, for moral support and discussions of many of the issues here.

An earlier version was published as "The Storrs Lectures: Behavioral Economics and Paternalism," 113 Yale L.J. 1826 (2013), and I am grateful to the editors of the *Yale Law Journal* for immensely valuable editorial suggestions and for permission to reprint material here. Some portions of the original lectures also appeared in *Simpler: The Future of Government* (Simon and Schuster, 2012), and I am grateful to Thomas LeBien for editorial help on that occasion.

Index

Index

149–51; and probability, 48–49
(*see also* probability judgment);
by public officials, 101–2, 120;
and reversibility, 152–53; and
salience, 40; short vs. long-
term, 28–29, 108; unrealistic
optimism, 44–48. *See also*
decision-making
System 2 thinking: about, 26–34;
and autonomy, 134; legitimate
claims, 154–59; privileging
over System 1, 157; promoting
through nudges, 149–51; and
the public domain, 100–101,
120–21; and salience, 40;
strengthening, 154. *See also*
decision-making

taxes: affective, 32–33; monetary,
29, 82, 111–12, 144, 147
texting while driving: bans, 19, 38,
56, 97–98, 124; educational
campaigns, 32, 33; graphic
warnings, 151; risk of harm to
others, 80; risks not weighed,
9, 45
time inconsistency, 35–36, 69–71
tools of paternalism, 53–55, 82–86,
139–41. *See also specific tools,
such as* default rules
transparency, 144–51

unrealistic optimism, 44–48,
63–64, 92–93
utility: decision vs. experienced
utility, 108–10; Mill's understanding of, 18, 72, 102–3 (*see
also* Mill, John Stuart); and
morality, 135–36, 184(n9).
See also welfare

Wallace, David Foster, 14, 132
warnings. *See* graphic warnings
Washington, George, 121
welfare: and autonomy, 123–29,
134, 136–38, 164; Bridge
Exception, 105–7, 109; defining, 71–75, 102–3; and
paternalism, 18–19, 21–23,
52–55, 70–71, 74–80, 87–88,
141; safety laws and, 97–98 (*see
also* seatbelts; texting while
driving). *See also* soft drinks
welfarist objections to paternalism,
91–102; arguments against,
102–13, 164, 181(n22); competition, 92–94, 113; Epistemic
Argument, 7, 21–22, 91–92; generally, 87–90; heterogeneity,
96–100, 114–15; learning,
94–96, 114; public choice and
bureaucratic behavior, 17,
100–102, 115, 117, 119–20

CCH

CCH

NOV 0 4 2015